THE GIANT

ORSON WELLES, THE ARTIST & THE SHADOW

YOUSSEF DAOUDI

23rd St.
New York

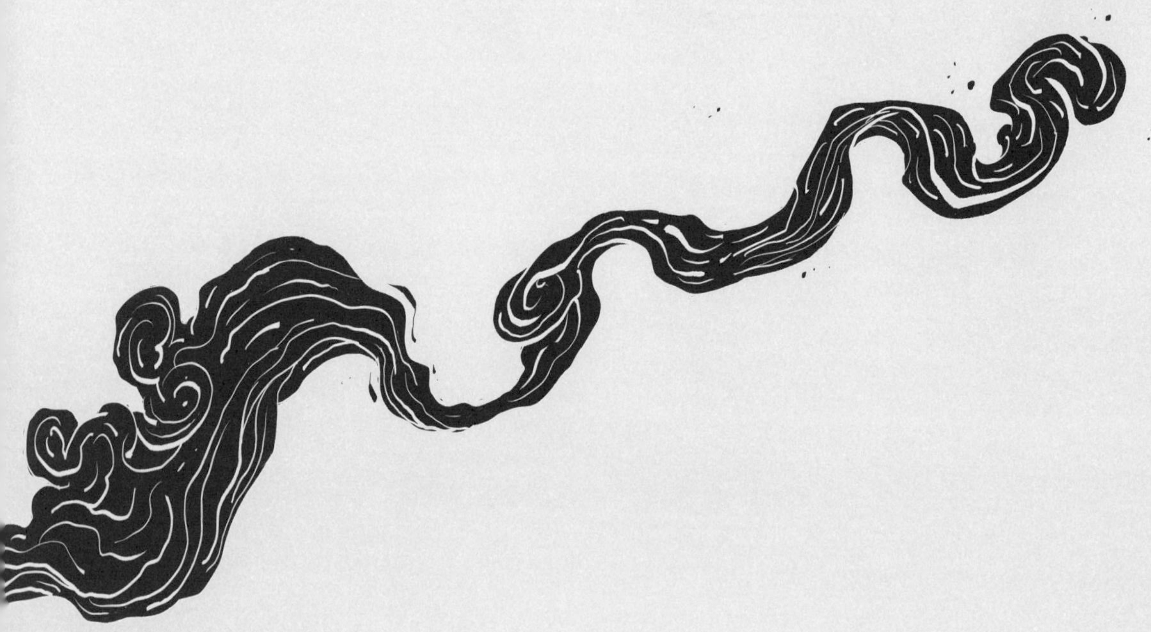

California
is a nice place
if you're
an orange

INT. THE STAGE - NIGHT

It used to be quite easy to hate this town. Easier than you might think.

For me, it was no trouble at all.

Still, that was many years ago...

...and while I don't think either of us have mellowed very much since then...

...we are getting on a bit, and our feelings for each other are scarcely as passionate as they were.

One thing didn't change...

...something is rotten in Tinseltown.

Yet I wouldn't mind raising its poisoned chalice to my lips one more time...

...one last time.

As long as people
stop asking questions
I will never be able
to answer...

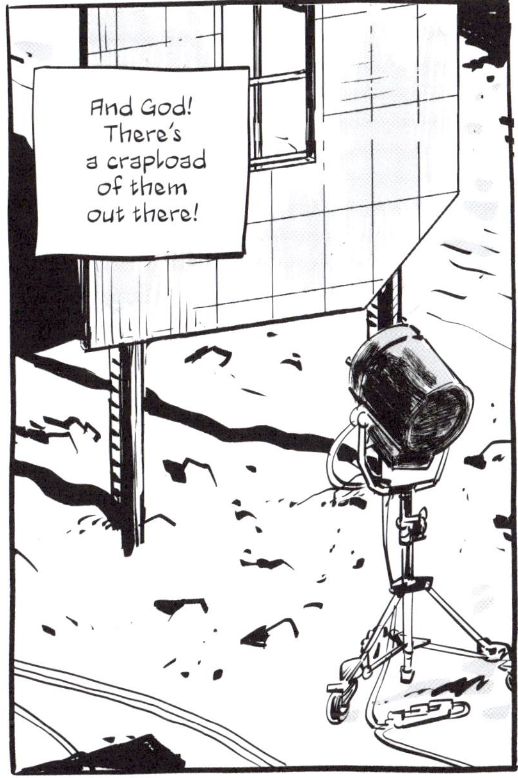
And God!
There's
a crapload
of them
out there!

However...I can
address the one
that's asked time
and again:

What ever
happened
to me?

Hehe...
Well, that's a good one.
HA!

MHA... HAHAHAHA! HEHEHE!

Nothing "happened"!

I've written, adapted, directed, and performed in some of the greatest works ever made...
I've traveled everywhere. I've drawn, painted, loved, and hated...
I can't count the number of things I did, good or bad.
I was never **FORGOTTEN.** Never sank into self-pity, bitterness, or obscurity, the way so many others did.
I hope not.
I **WILL** not.

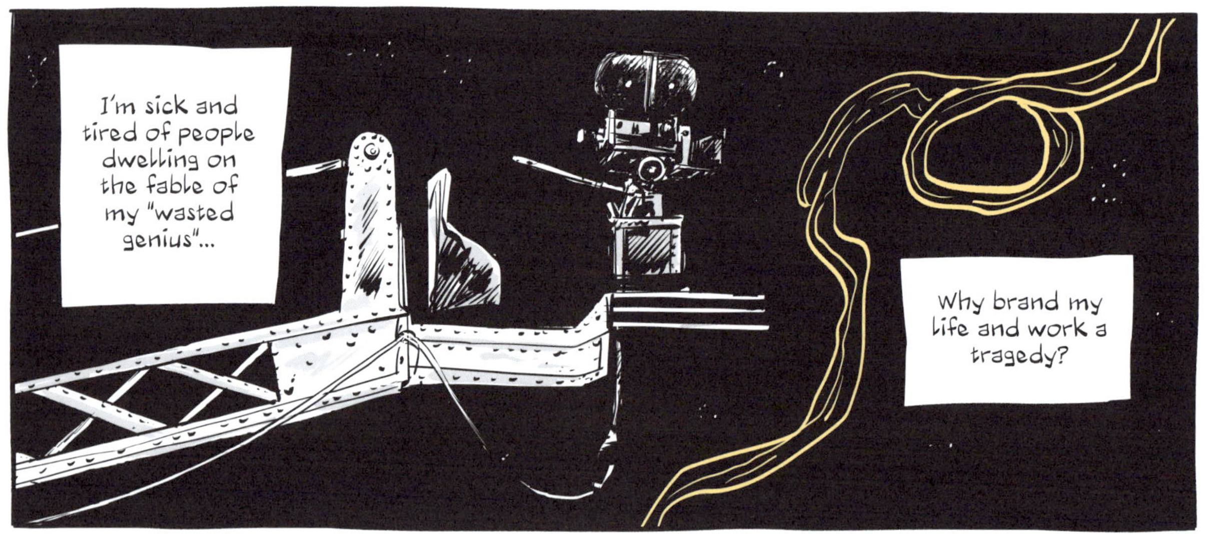
I'm sick and tired of people dwelling on the fable of my "wasted genius"...
Why brand my life and work a tragedy?

Please, don't you worry about that.

To my knowledge, I don't glow in the dark.

I'm still in the game. I can still say "action" and "cut" just like all the other fellas!

Hell! I can even act in a comic book!

No, ladies and gentlemen, nothing happened. And I have news for you...
...I'm back in town, and I want a rematch.

I'm Orson Welles.
HOLLYWOOD

The Pitch

1977

EXT. HOLLYWOOD - DAY

You don't ever want to open a play at the top of your bent, but **A MOVIE** should open at the top of its bent.
CALIFORNIA REPUBLIC

It must—because the damn screen is dead. It's a projected image, and you cannot bring the thing alive unless you seize the people at the beginning.
The riderless horse has to come in.
Restaurant PICARD
Ma Maison
Bistrot PICARD

Back to the story. We're here to talk about my movie, right?
At its inception, it was supposed to be about bullfighting and the fascination with death and ruin... A kind of portrait of decadence.
MA MAISON
BISTROT
PRESSE FRANÇAISE
VILLE DE PARIS
LICENCE
DEBIT DE BOISSONS
Ici Paris

J. J. Hannaford, the man who died in the accident, is an aging movie director. Imagine a sort of pseudo-Hemingway.

INT. "MA MAISON" RESTAURANT - NIGHT

That's the movie I want to make.
Or, rather, finish making...
...with your help, of course.

There are so many themes here.
Read the script. It's quite amazing.
Very intriguing.

The Other Side of the Wind. How beautiful is that!
I very much like that title too.

It oozes with mystery.

The original title was *Sacred Beasts*, until I transmuted the plot to be about **HOLLYWOOD** instead of bullfighting.
Who's the lead?

My old friend John Huston. Who else?
He's great, and the rest of the cast too.
Paul Stewart...
Susan Strasberg...
Norman Foster...
Lilli Palmer...
Edmond O'Brien...
Oh! And Peter Bogdanovich and Dennis Hopper, two promising actors and directors... All terrific professionals.
This is gonna be **A HIT!**
We'll be glad to secure the funding as soon as possible, Mr. Welles...
...Absolutely, provided that things are settled with your previous backers.
They are.
I have relinquished more than fifty percent of my rights to them. Don't you worry about them.
Believe me, they couldn't be happier.
Who wouldn't be, working with the man who made *Citizen Kane*?
GROWL!

GROO
WAF!

WAF WIF WIF
WIF WAF
WAF! WOF

You don't wanna bite my future producers, little one. It'd be a VERY BAD IDEA!

Now, be quiet and let the adults talk.
WOF!
Hush!

You are aware that I've made a few pictures since THAT ONE.
Of course, Mr. Welles. And I have an all-time personal favorite: The Magnificent Ambersons...

THAT'S WHAT I'M TALKING ABOUT!

FROM THE MAN WHO MADE "THE BEST PICTURE OF 1941"
It is my favorite too, **BY FAR!** ...At least the version I had in mind...
ORSON WELLES'
MERCURY PRODUCTION OF BOOTH TARKINGTON'S GREAT NOVEL
THE MAGNIFICENT AMBERSONS
...before they literally **BUTCHERED** it...
It was a **MUCH BETTER** picture than *Kane*...
WROF!

...if they'd just left it as it was.

Such a waste...

A quarter of a century ago, on my own and free of the crippling restraints of the Hollywood factory system, I managed to make a couple of pictures.
Ambersons was the second of these.
Paramount Pictures
What's surprising is that I lasted in the business as long as I did.

In those days, the movie industry was making a very successful product for a middle-aged, middle-class, middlebrow market.

Nowadays, the only thing the bosses know is that the market is very young.

So what's their solution? Give very young filmmakers total control of their own work.

NEW HOLLYWOOD
(THE MOVIE BRATS)

Bob Rafelson

Peter Bogdanovich

Martin Scorsese

Mike Nichols

Robert Altman

Francis Ford Coppola

Like a nervous old lady, Hollywood is suddenly afraid of the traffic. She needs youthful hands to guide her!

This trust is rather touching, slightly ridiculous, and very hopeful for the future of American films.

Ouvert de Midi à Minuit
Tel: 655.1991

Ma Maison
Restaurant-Bistrot
8368 Melrose av.

Sales Taxes will be added to retail price of all taxable items
Not responsible for lost or stolen articles.

Soupe Bloody Mary 1.25
Tomato Soup with a touch of Vodka
Soupe Avgolemono 1.25
Chicken Soup with eggs and Lemon Sauce

Quiche Lorraine 1.50
Homemade Cheese Tart
Crabes aux Artichauts 2.00
Artichoke Hearts Baked with Crab Meat
Sardines à l'Huile 1.25
Sardines in Olive Oil
Our Homemade Country Style Paté
Avocats au Tarama (en saison) 1.75
Avocado Topped with Sauce Taram and Greek Caviar

Salades
Salade de Cresson 1.75
Watercress, Tomato
Salade d'Epinard Mimosa 2.00
mushrooms, Chopped Eggs

Grillades
Entrecôte Grillée 7.95
Steak New-York

Croque-Madame
Fried Turkey Swiss Cheese

6.75 Brochet
6.25 Pouletaux
Chicken served with Orange Sauce
6.00 Crêpes aux Fruits de Mer 6.00
Seafood Crepe.

I still have that greedy need to exercise, in some way, the function of my choice: the function of director.

I feel young and strong...

and hungry!

Aren't you?

Oh, sure!

Yeah! Looking at this mouthwatering menu..

The chef is the real thing. Wolfgang Puck.

Bonjour! What shall we have today?
Ah! Patrick!
I'm counting on you to provide my guests with a proper introduction to California's *nouvelle cuisine*.
Avec plaisir!
Mr. Terrail comes from a proud lineage of first-rate *restaurateurs*.
Just like his uncle who runs the famous Tour d'Argent in Paris. I had so many wonderful meals there when I was shooting *The Trial*.
Well, Ma Maison is a little bit of Paris in Melrose...
...and what we try to do here is very simple: We use natural, locally grown, fresh ingredients to produce our lightly cooked dishes.
Talking about movies always makes me hungry.
Bon, d'accord...
You'll tell Wolfgang to go easy on the capers?
Okay?
What's the dish of the day?
The sole meunière, madame.
I love the meunière!
I'm tempted by the chicken...

...I'm having the *salade.*
You see, my doctor told me recently to stop having intimate dinners for four...
Salade greco
Romaine, ice
Salade de R
Brown Ri
2.00
Filet de Sc
Filet

...unless there are **THREE** other people.
MHA! HAHAHAHA!

MHA HAHAHAHAHA! HUHUHAHAHAHAHA!
I'd recognize that gargantuan laugh anywhere.
Is he ever going to finish any of his movies?
Orson, you old dog!
Now that's pitching.
Those two producers!
Poor bastards.
Restaurant PICARD Ma Maison Bistrot PICARD

HAHA!
Orson is in the house, huh?
And he's hungry.

Nothing like a good Meursault to celebrate.

Here's to you.
Thank you for helping an aging director make one last picture before he's completely superseded by the new guard.
I'm talking about Hannaford, the character... **OBVIOUSLY.**

Wunderkind

1915

INT. WELLES' RESIDENCE - NIGHT

But in the younger one, she finds the perfect subject for her experiment.

Very good, Orson. Keep going.
The tempo!
Andante!

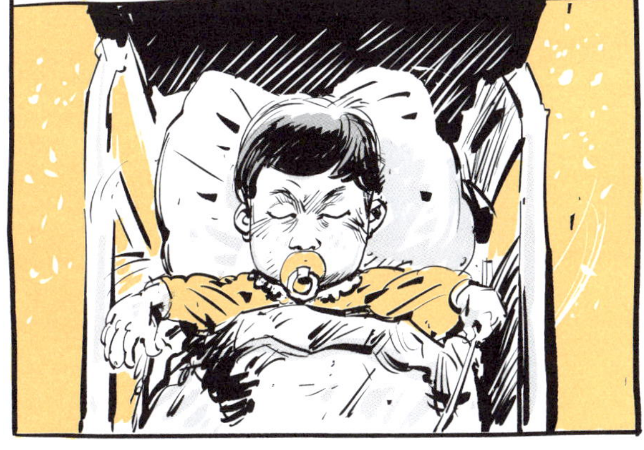
The father, Richard Welles, is not home. The marriage deteriorated over irreconciliable differences that grew over time.

He is presumably off carousing—drinking, gambling, and otherwise squandering his fortune.

Enter Dr. Maurice Bernstein, Beatrice's physician.

A brilliant surgeon, a sophisticated socialite, and a man of taste.

Maurice!

How are you feeling today?
You've done me such good, you wouldn't believe it.
I'm glad the medicine is working.
YOU ARE my medicine, Maurice.
What about Pookles, is he taking his drops?
The desire to take medicine is one of the greatest features which distinguishes men from animals.
This is a very blessed child, Beatrice.
Oh, there's still room for progress.

Children could be treated as adults as long as they were amusing.
YES!
WHAT A TALENT!
MARVELOUS!
BRAVO!
The moment they became boring, it was off to the nursery.

For years, this boy never heard a word of discouragement.

He painted, and they said, "Nobody's ever painted like that," you know?
OOH!
MASTERPIECE!

He played, and they said, "Nobody's ever played like that!"
KWEEE!
KWEEK!

He wrote, and they said, "Nobody's ever written so well as that!"

He did magic tricks, and they said, "Here's the new Houdini!"
BRAVO!
BRAVO!

It seemed to him that there was no limit to what he could do!
BRILLIANT!
MERAVIGLIOSO!
He didn't know what was waiting for him, poor thing.
BRAVO!

At school, he was regarded as a freak by adults and children alike...
I don't think that child is normal.
Well, he's a wunderkind.
I wouldn't want him in my classroom.
THE FRENCH REVOLUTION
HEY! WELLES!
Tales from Shake
STOP READING, ORSON!
WHITMAN
His mother is an intellectual. She has a lover and all.
Where's her husband?
You think you're smart, huh?
THEATER
COMMEDIA dell'ARTE
Come and play ball with us! Reading is for sissies!
Richard Welles is some kind of inventor. He must be somewhere spending his estate on booze and gambling.

At a very early age, the boy was immersed in the cosmopolitan salons of the intellectual elite, particularly after moving to Chicago. He mastered language, syntax, and vocabulary, and would often engage in verbal jousts with adults.

A stage aficionado himself, Maurice Bernstein would have a lifelong influence on the child.
One of his earliest and most notable gifts to Orson was a puppet theater.
Orson wrote dialogue, made puppets, and provided them with dozens of voices, like a seasoned ventriloquist.
Orson's Guignol
Later, Dr. Bernstein helped Orson turn the attic into a miniature theater using packing crates and window shades.
Over time, the attic became so jam-packed with dramatic paraphernalia, props, masks, fragments of costumes, and jars of makeup, that it came to look like the backstage of a real theater.

Living permanently with Beatrice, Dr. Bernstein became implicitly the boy's surrogate father, to the immense ire of Richard Welles.

Dadda says it takes a lot of work to become one, Daddy.

Yeah, whatever.

Can't he call you Orson like everybody else?

By the way, where does Orson come from?

When the boy
was nine years old,
Beatrice Welles died.

His pain was so intense that he decided the only way to escape it was to escape childhood itself.

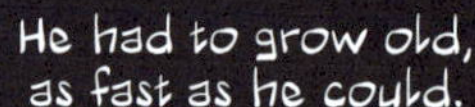

In his mind, he was already a grown man. He simply needed to look the part.

Maybe a wig, a bit of makeup, a nose, and facial hair would do the trick.

And cigars should make his voice mature quicker than nature would allow.

It's time to enter the stage. The stage of fools and old, tormented kings...

BLOW, WINDS, AND CRACK YOUR CHEEKS!
YOU CATARACTS AND HURRICANOES, SPOUT TILL YOU HAVE DRENCH'D OUR STEEPLES, DROWN'D THE COCKS!
You sulphurous and thought-executing fires, vaunt-couriers to oak-cleaving thunderbolts, singe my white head!
RAGE!
Here I stand your slave!
A poor, infirm, weak, and despis'd old man.
BLOW!
That will with two pernicious daughters join your high-engender'd battles 'gainst a head so old and white as this!
O! O! 'TIS FOUL!
BRAVO!
YES!
WHAT A TALENT!

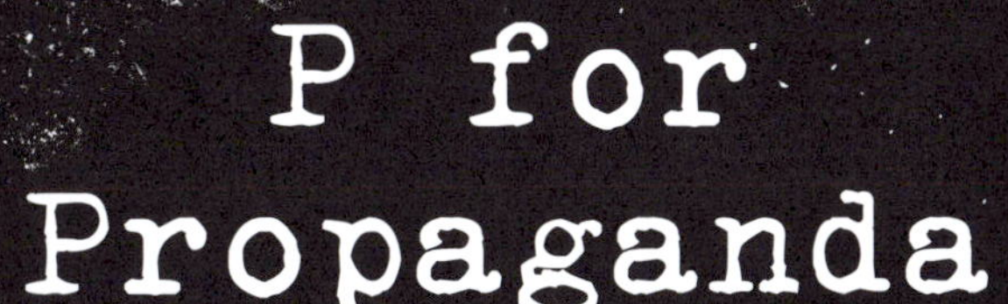

1938

INT. MERCURY THEATRE - NIGHT

The Ides of March are come.

SPEAK, HANDS, FOR ME!

Et tu, Brute?

Then fall, Caesar!

...If then that friend demand why Brutus rose against Caesar, this is my answer:
Not that I loved Caesar less, but that **I LOVED ROME MORE.**

Had you rather Caesar were living, and die all slaves, than that Caesar were dead, to live all free men?

As Caesar loved me, I weep for him; as he was fortunate, I rejoice at it; as he was valiant, I honor him...
...but, as he was ambitious...
... I SLEW HIM.

There is tears for his love...
...joy for his fortune...
...honor for his valor...

...and DEATH, for his ambition.

YES!
BRAVO!
YES!
BRAVO!

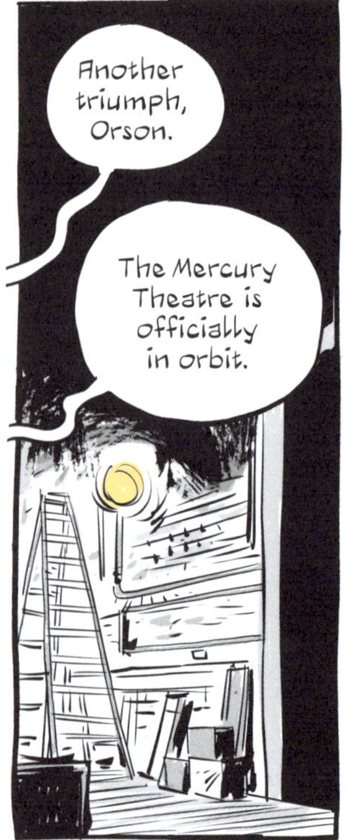
Another triumph, Orson.
The Mercury Theatre is officially in orbit.

The Campbell Soup folks would like to talk, right after the *Shadow* broadcast.
Perfect. Let's eat with them as soon as possible.

We need a big fat sponsor for all the stuff we have planned.
The company has to be renamed...
"Campbell Soup on the Air," there you go...

I'll write my lines for tonight's episode on the way.
Our ride is here!
An ambulance?
BELL AMBULANCE
MERCUR
PRESENTS
JULIUS CAESAR

WUP!
I have no time for taxis.

WUUUUU WUWUWU
BELL
AMBULANCE

Do you ever sleep?
I get it, John, I'm doing too many things at once. But it's nothing compared with my time at the Todd School. I could stay awake for weeks back then.
WUP!
GENTLEMEN
ROSES

Maybe I'm gettin' old.
Old? You're barely twenty-three!

Yet your theatrical experience is already greater and richer than mine.

WUUUUU WUWUWU
And you may have the most valuable thing: AN INNATE DRAMATIC INSTINCT.

But what's even more amazing is that you seem to feel yourself, at all times, to be the rightful and undisputed master of that art.
HAHA!

You sound like you're in love, my friend. I'm a happily married man! HAHAHAHA!

Okay. Tell me about your project...

I'd like to do something different. I doubt it's ever been done before...

Everything you do is...
Imagine the normal radio broadcast interrupted by late-breaking news bulletins.

The idea is to do it in such a realistic fashion that a crisis would actually seem to be happening...
BELL AMBULANCE
An invasion would be perfect.
The Germans.
The little mustachioed madman wouldn't mind, John.
No. Not the Nazis.
We gotta find a work we can adapt for this, something outlandish...
...It must SOUND real.
Science fiction? An interplanetary crisis.
AN INVASION FROM OUTER SPACE!

The Columbia Broadcasting System and its affiliated stations present:

With infinite complacence, people went to and fro over the earth about their little affairs, serene in the assurance of their dominion over this small, spinning fragment of solar driftwood...
...Yet across an immense ethereal gulf, minds that are to our minds as ours are to the beasts in the jungle...
CBS
...regarded this earth with envious eyes and slowly and surely drew their plans against us.
In the thirty-ninth year of the twentieth century came THE GREAT DISILLUSIONMENT.

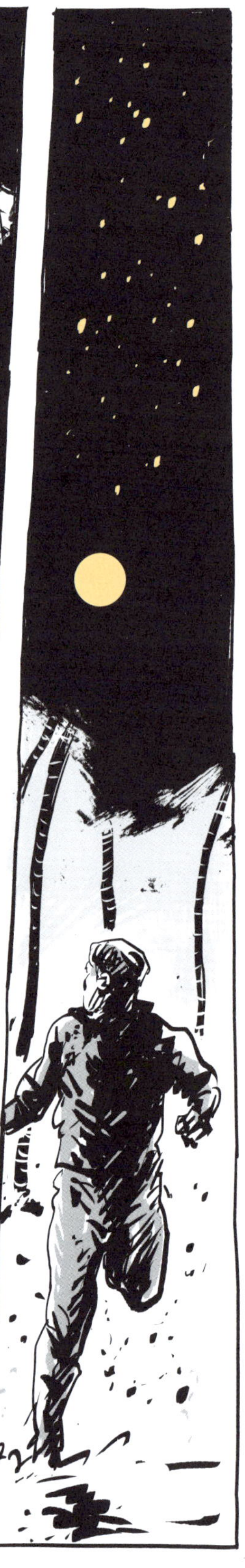

They made a whole fuss about a nationwide panic.

Some myths
are hard
to bust,
I guess.

CBS
I can understand
if a few people
were spooked.

The most terrifying
thing is suddenly
becoming aware
that we are
not alone.

But the whole business unveiled something far more important.
Radio in those days, before the tube and everything thereafter, wasn't just a noise in somebody's pocket.
Shoo!
Radio was a voice of authority.
Too much so.

DON'T YOU DARE TOUCH MY CIGAR!

The rest is history.

Your father has become a household name now.
I can do whatever I want.
The folks in Hollywood are all chasing me.
Louis B. Mayer himself is offering me a job.
But I'm signing with RKO. I like the studio, and George Schaefer is a nice fellow.
I can fulfill my dream...
You hear me, Darling Girl?
The dream of a lifetime.
THE MOVIES!

HOLLYWOOD

Heart of Darkness is the quintessence of first-person singular. I want that translated into film.

We'll use a subjective camera—the experience will be absolutely unique.

I want the spectator to be in Marlow's shoes, have Marlow's eyes, as he goes deeper and deeper into the darkest confines of the jungle and the human soul.
THE HORROR!
THE HORROR!

Everything is ready: the storyboards, the props, even the poster.
CONCEPT

Great work from the art department, right?
ORSON WELLES
HEART OF DARKNESS

Orson, we've given you an awfully long leash for a newbie, but this picture is way over budget.
Besides, I was expecting a boy-meets-girl kinda story here...
It is one!

Marlow is in love with a girl...
...and there's a hell of an adventure going up the river.
There are cannibals, shootings, petty bickerings, native dances, a fascinating black girl...

Come on, George, I shot my bolt on preproduction for this picture. I can never do such elaborate work again...
You're still young, and such a talented fellow, you'll make many movies. But not this one.
KURTZ

You gotta finish that script you're writing with Mankiewicz. I'm ready to sell that one to the board.
Yeah.

And, Orson, get rid of the damn beard, will you?
This beard here? You know I was planning to play Kurtz.

Your facial hair makes us look bad. Every exec, critic, and their mother takes it as an intolerable provocation.
KING KON
FAY WRAY • ROBT. AR
BRUCE CABOT
EDGAR WALLACE

Oh, I see. The bearded intellectual is the new bogeyman.

I thought Hollywood was the whisker capital of the nation!
For heaven's sake, there are fellows out on the streets with muttonchops growing past their shoulders, riding carts drawn by zebras. Nobody bats an eye.
People take **YOUR** beard personally, son.

This is some funny place, George.

There's still a lot you have to learn about this town, Orson.
R.K.O RADIO PICTURES INC
R K O

I hope everything is to your satisfaction, Mr. Welles?
NO ADMITTANCE
THIS STAGE MUST BE KEPT LOCKED AT ALL TIMES

This is the biggest electric train set a boy ever had!
Mr. Welles, you're not any boy, you're **A WONDER BOY.**
The studio is betting big on you.

I'm giving
it my all.
And I have the
best cameraman
in the business.

No, no,
everybody's
expecting
something
grand.
You
understand,
Mr. Welles?

After all,
you're a genius.

So start filming!
Be a genius.

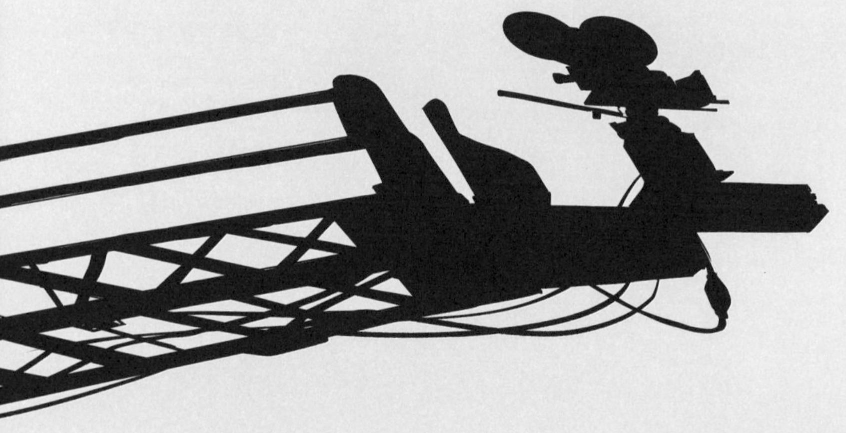

The Greatest Movie Ever Made

1940

INT. THE STAGE - NIGHT

From the very beginning, I was seen as this young... terrible maverick...

This beatnik, this guy with a beard who was going to do it all by himself.

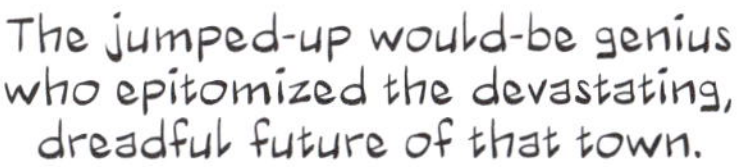
The jumped-up would-be genius who epitomized the devastating, dreadful future of that town.

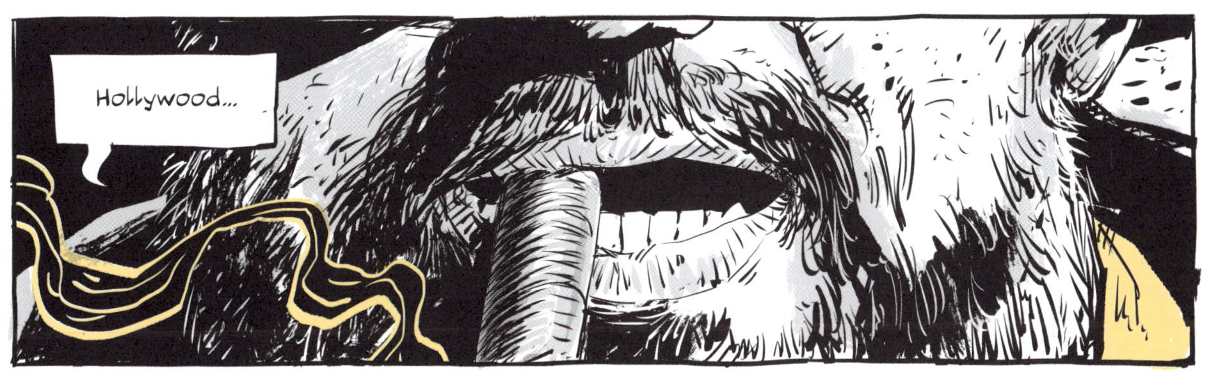
Hollywood...

But in Tinseltown, careers are fleeting, elusive, illusive...
They're done and undone quicker than you think...

...Faster than a sleight-of-hand trick...

Like magic...
CLIC!

KRRRRRRRR...

BOM! TARIITATA TARATATAAA!

THIS IS...

MARCH OF THE NEWS

...MARCH OF THE NEWS!

October 30, 1938. Who spread a wave of mass hysteria with a too-realistic dramatization of H. G. Wells's *The War of the Worlds*?

DAILY

FAKE RADIO 'WAR' STIRS TERROR THROUGH U.S.

All crashed...

Who is this young man with the perfectly modulated, cavernous voice?

MUAHAHAHA! WHO KNOWS WHAT EVIL LURKS IN THE HEARTS OF MEN? THE SHADOW KNOWS! MUAHAHAHA!

Who sends cold shivers racing up your spine in his famous broadcasts as Lamont Cranston, the millionaire playboy and vigilante?

...THIS MAN IS MR. ORSON WELLES, THE BOY WONDER FROM KENOSHA, WISCONSIN!

Cartoonist, Actor, Poet and only 10

Orson G. Welles
—Photo by De Longe

A POET, artist, cartoonist, and actor at 10 years old.

Orson G. Welles, a pupil in the fourth grade at the Washington school, is already attracting the attention of some of the greatest literary men and artists in the country.

As young as he may be, Orson Welles's career on the stage began a long time ago. At only three years old, he made his first theater appearance in Puccini's *Madama Butterfly*.

At sixteen, the prodigy set out on a painting tour of Ireland with $500, traveling by donkey cart. He ended up at the Gate Theatre in Dublin, where he posed as a Broadway star and received his first professional part, in *Jew Süss*.

The applause was thunderous, and totally unexpected.

I got more acclaim for that than for anything I've done since.

Today, he is one of the best-paid entertainers in the country. Star of innumerable radio broadcasts and brilliant director of the Mercury Theatre, a groundbreaking company founded with his associate John Houseman.

His early collaboration with the Federal Theatre Project* in 1935 as both director and actor established Welles as a major force in American theater.

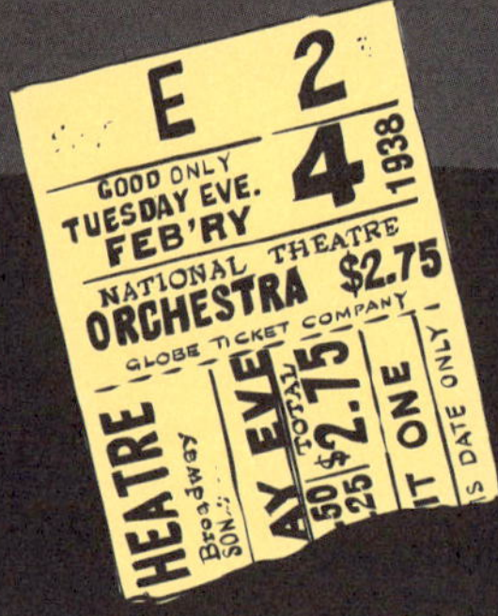

One of the most remarkable creations of that era was his *Macbeth*, also known as the *Voodoo Macbeth*, which featured an all-black cast.

*The Federal Theatre Project (FTP) was a New Deal program that provided work for unemployed theater professionals during the Great Depression.

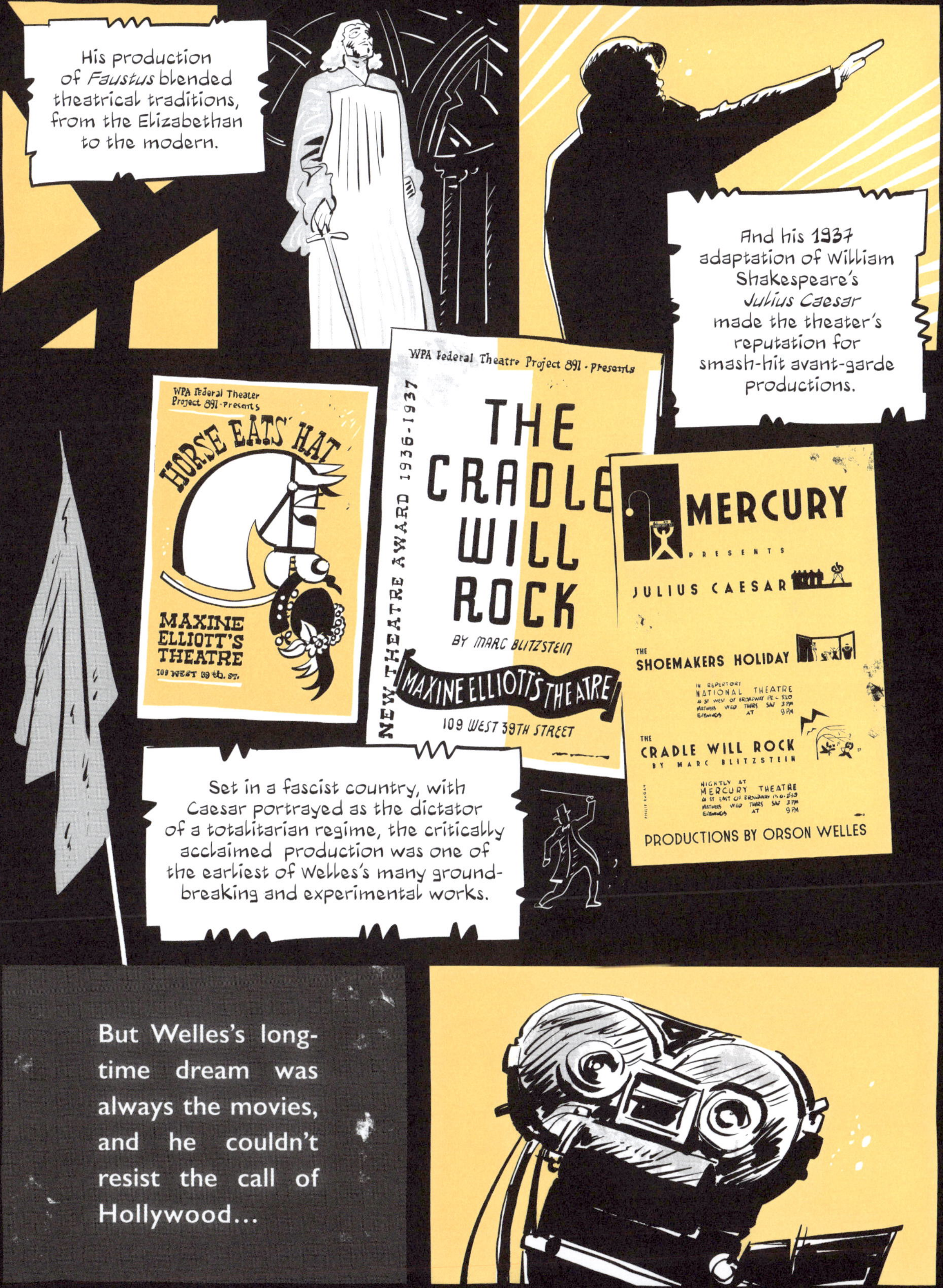

His production of *Faustus* blended theatrical traditions, from the Elizabethan to the modern.

And his 1937 adaptation of William Shakespeare's *Julius Caesar* made the theater's reputation for smash-hit avant-garde productions.

WPA Federal Theater Project 891 - Presents
HORSE EATS HAT
MAXINE ELLIOTT'S THEATRE
109 WEST 39th. ST.

WPA Federal Theatre Project 891 - Presents
THE CRADLE WILL ROCK
BY MARC BLITZSTEIN
MAXINE ELLIOTT'S THEATRE
109 WEST 39TH STREET
NEW THEATRE AWARD 1936-1937

MERCURY
PRESENTS
JULIUS CAESAR
THE SHOEMAKERS HOLIDAY
IN REPERTORY
NATIONAL THEATRE

PRODUCTIONS BY ORSON WELLES

Set in a fascist country, with Caesar portrayed as the dictator of a totalitarian regime, the critically acclaimed production was one of the earliest of Welles's many groundbreaking and experimental works.

But Welles's longtime dream was always the movies, and he couldn't resist the call of Hollywood...

At twenty-four, Orson Welles signed an extraordinary contract with RKO Pictures, allowing him to write, produce, direct, and act in his own films, with final cut and approval over all aspects of the production.
It was widely considered the most generous contract ever given to a Hollywood newcomer.

Welles was interested in creating a film that would break with the traditional Hollywood model. He hired veteran screenwriter Herman Mankiewicz to help him develop the script for *Citizen Kane*.

BEEP BIP BEEP BIP
An RKO Picture
BIP BEEP BEEP BIP
BIP BEEP BIP
BEEP BIP BEEP
BEEP BEEP BEEP

ROSEBUD

A story of hubris,
power and corruption,
memory and identity...
love and betrayal.

KANE

A critique of the
American dream...
How it can be corrupted
by greed and ambition.
How it can lead to
isolation and loneliness.

The fictional Charles Foster Kane was largely inspired by real-life media magnate William Randolph Hearst. Welles drew heavily from Hearst's life, relationships, and career.

And I don't like that.

The film shows Kane's lavish lifestyle and delusions of grandeur embodied in the megalomaniacal Xanadu estate, which bears an eerie resemblance to Hearst Castle in San Simeon, California.
Even more loathsome to Hearst and his allies was the portrayal of Kane's second wife, a young alcoholic singer with strong parallels to Hearst's mistress, the showgirl-turned-actress Marion Davies.
The Daily Chronicle
EXTRA
CANDIDATE KANE CAUGHT IN LOVE NEST WITH "SINGER"
THE HIGHLY MORAL MR. KANE AND HIS TAME "SONGBIRD"
Entrapped By Wife As Love Pirate, Kane Refuses to Quit Race
Susan Alexander Revealed As Woman Nesting With Publisher While He Was Prating About Morality
Actress Dorothy Comingore was a dead ringer for Marion Davies.
EXTRA
Red scum!

Long before *Citizen Kane* premiered, Hearst began a series of brutal attacks on Welles in his newspapers, and barred his publications from running advertisements for the film.

Bay Region Leaders Acclaim Mr. Hearst's Speech Denouncing Communis

LAWMAKERS

TYRANNY OPPOSED

Outspoken Analysis of Soviet Rule Called Timely Warning

'KEYNOTE OF AMERICANISM'

EXPOSE SEEN AS BLOW TO PROPAGANDA

SOVIET YULE CELEBRATED AMID SQUALOR

Christmas Eve of Old Russian Calendar Observed by Poor, Replaces pre-Revolt Grandeur

THE PRESIDENT'S MESSAGE

dissipated by inefficiency, or stolen in the usual method of political crookedness.

THE Administration seems to have delusions of grandeur.

When they have good ideas,—and that is quite frequently—they propose them, and perhaps endeavor to execute them, on such a scale that they defeat their object.

An enormous number of bureaus are created; an enormous amount of government employes

Summary Day's Ne

It seems you don't like my picture, *Citizen Kane*, Mr. Hearst. I understand you haven't even seen it.

I know who you are, Welles. A communist.

It's Terrific!

If you had, I think you would agree with me that those who have advised you that "Kane" is Hearst have done us both an injustice.

Hollywood is full of them these days—immigrants and refugees from Europe, taking film jobs from real Americans.

CITIZEN WELLES VS CITIZEN HEARST

Just watch the movie. It's quite nice.

I will destroy you.

JOSEPH COTTEN · DOROTHY COMINGORE · EVERETT SLOANE · RAY COLLINS · GEORGE COULOURIS
AGNES MOOREHEAD · PAUL STEWART · RUTH WARRICK · ERSKINE SANFORD · WILLIAM ALLAND

Meet ORSON WELLES Columnist

On stage, screen or on the air, Orson Welles has always made headlines. Now he writes them in an instructive, entertaining, mirth-provoking commentary on outstanding personalities, current news and coming events. Read "Orson Welles' Almanac" daily.

STARTS MONDAY, JAN 22ND

New York Post
55 West 43 Street, New York 15, N. Y.

The Hearst papers have repeatedly described me as a communist. I am not a communist. I am grateful for our constitutional form of government, and I rejoice in our great American tradition of democracy.

Deport the Alien Reds! Rescind the Recognition Of Soviet Russia!

THE fact that Communism—nurtured by Soviet Russia—is seeking to destroy the free institutions of America is not to be denied.

Neither is the shameful fact to be denied that COMMUNISTS are supporting Franklin D. Roosevelt for re-election in 1936 IN ORDER TO BUILD A REVOLUTIONARY "PEOPLES FRONT" IN 1940.

Mr. Roosevelt has said that he repudiates this support.

But what has he done to prove that he repudiates it?

Russian Communism in America can be officially repudiated only by two courses of executive action:

1—By immediately deporting all alien communists, as the law requires; and

2—By immediately rescinding the recognition of Soviet Russia.

Hearst's ire became even greater when Welles wrote and starred in a radio play that represented everything he hated and despised.

Welles's personal views, especially in regards to politics, racism, communism, and religion, are expressed in this story about life in a small Texas border town. Hearst papers attacked the radio program, calling it "propaganda worthy of Moscow."

Hearst orchestrated a communist witch hunt against Welles. Shortly before the premiere of *Citizen Kane*, the FBI opened a file on Welles containing a list of his associations with organizations that were supposedly "communist in character," from the League of American Writers to the Foster Parents' Plan for War Children, a food relief organization for kids whose lives were disrupted by war.

HUAC

House Un-American Activities Commitee

The Free Company broadcasts are subversive in nature and definitely communistic in aims, although camouflaged by constant reference to democracy and free speech.

The Federal Theatre Project has done more to spread communist propaganda than the Communist Party itself!

A good tax adjustment should settle him down.

The evidence before us leads inevitably to the conclusion that the film *Citizen Kane* is nothing more than an extension of the Communist Party's campaign to smear Mr. Hearst, one of its most effective and consistent opponents in the United States.

The release of *Citizen Kane* in 1941 was met with mixed reactions from audiences and critics, and its immediate commercial success was limited. In fact, RKO lost $150,000 on it. The film was nominated for nine Academy Awards, but only won for Best Original Screenplay, losing Best Picture to *How Green Was My Valley*.

Welles begins production on the second picture of his three-picture RKO contract: *The Magnificent Ambersons*, based on the Pulitzer Prize–winning 1918 novel by Booth Tarkington.

Nearly half of the film's stars—Joseph Cotten, Agnes Moorehead, Ray Collins, and Erskine Sanford—were Mercury Theatre alumni. Welles himself provided the narration.

The story is about the declining fortunes of a wealthy midwestern family and the social changes brought by the automobile age.

In that town, in those days, all the women who wore silk or velvet knew all the other women who wore silk or velvet, and everybody knew everybody else's family horse-and-carriage.

The Daily Chronicle

EXTRA

U.S. DECLARES WAR

CONGRESS TO ACT QUICKLY IN REPLY TO JAPANESE ATTACK

With war raging in Europe and the Pacific, Welles answers another call—the call of duty. A goodwill tour of South America.

For this mission, Welles was commissioned by the State Department and Nelson Rockefeller, who was then serving as the Coordinator of Inter-American Affairs.

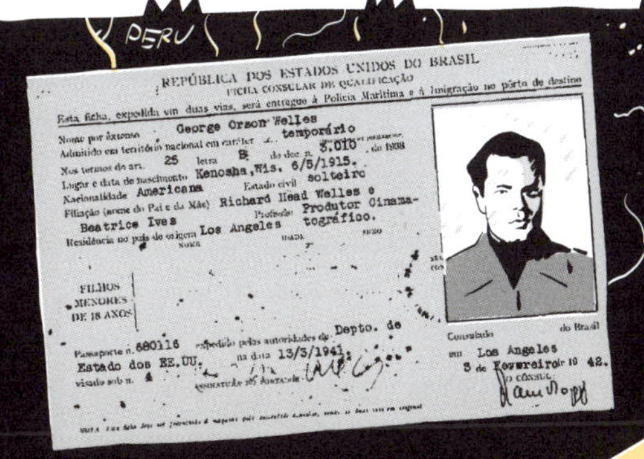

REPÚBLICA DOS ESTADOS UNIDOS DO BRASIL
FICHA CONSULAR DE QUALIFICAÇÃO

Esta ficha, expedida em duas vias, será entregue à Policia Maritima e à Imigração no pôrto de destino

Nome por extenso George Orson Welles
Admitido em territorio nacional em caráter temporário
Nos termos do art. 25 letra B do dec. n. 3.010 de 1938
Lugar e data de nascimento Kenosha, Wis. 6/5/1915.
Nacionalidade Americana Estado civil solteiro
Filiação (nome do Pai e da Mãe) Richard Head Welles e Beatrice Ives
Profissão Produtor Cinematográfico.
Residência no país de origem Los Angeles

FILHOS MENORES DE 18 ANOS

Passaporte n. 680116 expedido pelas autoridades do Depto. de Estado dos EE.UU. na data 13/3/1941.
visado sob n. 4

Consulado do Brasil em Los Angeles
3 de Fevereiro de 1942.
O CONSUL

The purpose of the tour was to improve relations between the United States and South American countries, and to promote cultural exchange.

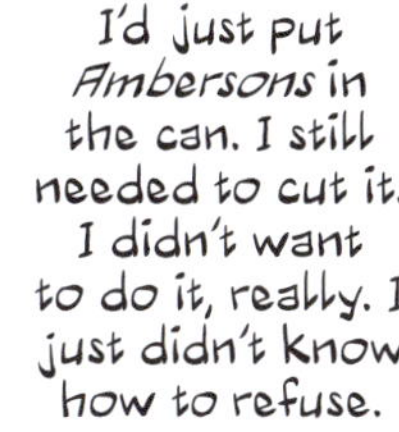

The project was called *It's All True*. How ironic that name would turn out to be.
The film was intended to showcase Latin American culture and society through four stories.
"The Story of Jazz" was intended to be a part of the project but was never filmed. This segment was meant to explore the history and cultural significance of jazz music, particularly its roots in African American culture in the United States.
From the sketchbook of Orson Welles
"The Story of Samba," or "Carnaval," was set in Rio de Janeiro, Brazil. It focused on the annual festival and featured a voodoo ceremony.
"My Friend Bonito" was set in Mexico and followed a young boy's journey to becoming a bullfighter.

"Four Men on a Raft" retold the grueling sea voyage that four impoverished Brazilian fishermen, or jangadeiros, had recently made to present, in person, their grievances to President Getúlio Vargas.
The script? There wasn't any!
You don't necessarily need a script, but you sure need a good story.
They ask to see the rushes of what I'm doing in South America. And they see a lot of people, black people, and the reaction is, "He's just shootin' a lot of colored yokels jumpin' up and down," you know?

What the hell is he doing down there?
Filming in some dirty and disreputable colored neighborhoods throughout the city.
RKO
R-K-O RADIO
He's spending **OUR** money cavorting with black women instead of finishing the damn film.
Orson Welles continued filming "Four Men on a Raft" while attempting to supervise the editing of *The Magnificent Ambersons* remotely.
Jacaré, the leader of the four jangadeiros, drowned while filming the reenactment of his epic voyage. A national hero, who had helped win union rights and pensions for poor fishermen throughout Brazil...
...killed by a goodwill picture.

Meanwhile, Welles's standing in Hollywood continued to deteriorate.

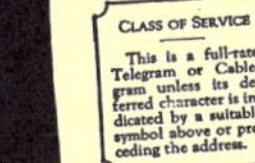

WESTERN UNION (95)

CLASS OF SERVICE: This is a full-rate Telegram or Cablegram unless its deferred character is indicated by a suitable symbol above or preceding the address.

SYMBOLS: DL=Day Letter; NL=Night Letter; LC=Deferred Cable; NLT=Cable Night Letter; Ship Radiogram

R. B. WHITE, PRESIDENT — NEWCOMB CARLTON, CHAIRMAN OF THE BOARD — J. C. WILLEVER, FIRST VICE-PRESIDENT

The filing time shown in the date line on telegrams and day letters is STANDARD TIME at point of origin. Time of receipt is STANDARD TIME at point of destination

MR154 63 LD RKO STUDIOS = LA, CA. VIA MEXICO CITY
1942 MAR 21 AM 11 43

ORSON WELLES

WE MUST HAVE A 'HEART TO HEART' TALK. YOU HAVE GOT TO DO SOMETHING COMMERCIAL. WE HAVE GOT TO GET AWAY FROM 'ARTY' PICTURES AND GET BACK TO EARTH. EDUCATING THE PEOPLE IS EXPENSIVE, AND YOUR NEXT PICTURE MUST BE MADE FOR THE BOX OFFICE. GOD KNOWS YOU HAVE ALL THE TALENT AND THE ABILITY FOR WRITING, PRODUCING, DIRECTING – EVERYTHING IN CITIZEN KANE AND AMBERSONS CONFIRMS THAT. WE SHOULD APPLY ALL THAT TALENT AND EFFORT IN THE RIGHT DIRECTION AND MAKE A PICTURE ON WHICH WE CAN GET WELL.

GEORGE SHAEFER

THE COMPANY WILL APPRECIATE SUGGESTIONS FROM ITS PATRONS CONCERNING ITS SERVICE

The final cut was drastically different from Welles's original vision, and it was released to poor reviews and box office returns.

They shot that mawkish ending without my knowledge or consent.

He was such a promising young fellow, but his career was nothing but a flash in the pan.

A would-be genius, nothing more.

RKO

Welles will not make another movie, not for my studio.

I don't want the Mercury people to set foot in here, ever!

You're fired, Welles!

Fired from RKO.

Fired from this movie.

YOU'RE FIRED FROM HOLLYWOOD ALTOGETHER!

1946. Orson Welles directed and starred in the highly anticipated Broadway musical production based on Jules Vernes's *Around the World in Eighty Days.*

ORSON WELLES

ARTHUR MARGETSON in

Around THE World

MUSIC AND LYRICS BY COLE PORTER

The production was extraordinarily costly, featuring a large cast, live animals, elaborate costumes, and innovative stage technology like rear-projection screens and rotating sets.

After running out of cash, Welles offered to write, direct, and star, with his then-wife Rita Hayworth, in a film for Columbia Pictures for just $55,000—the cost of *Around the World*'s costumes.

MUSICAL EXTRAVAGANZA

The musical closed after two months. It was a financial disaster.

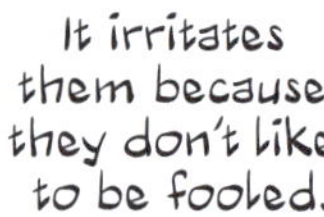
I know you hate magic. All women do.
It irritates them because they don't like to be fooled.

I don't know about the others, but, yes, I don't like that.

Rita...

...I wouldn't fool you for the world.
ORSON WELLES
The LADY from SHANGHAI
RITA HAYWORTH
BOM! TARIITATA TARATATAAA!

I shuffled around Hollywood for a few years after *Ambersons*, but my career there was over the moment I committed to finishing *It's All True.*

I had no choice **BUT** to finish it. I owed it to the jangadeiros, I owed it to poor Jacaré. I owed it to myself.

That was the real turning point in my story with Hollywood.

After I was fired, RKO developed a new motto, printed on every piece of paper the studio sent out...

RKO STUDIOS INC.

780 GOWER STREET, LOS ANGELES, CALIF.

Showmanship Instead of Genius

I came to Hollywood thinking that I would be lucky if they let me do a second picture.

They didn't.
They just hated me passionately for having committed the unthinkable:

...A MASTERPIECE.

What's worse is that I might have done it too early.

As I always say...
...I started at the top...
...and have been working my way down ever since.
ORSON WELLES
It's Terrific
ORSON WELLES CITIZEN KANE
ORSON WELLES CITIZEN KANE

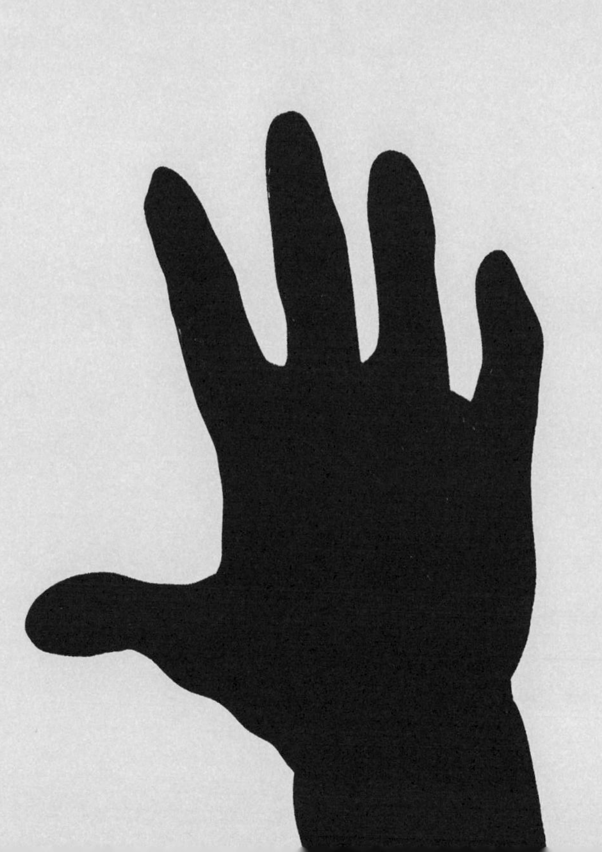

Thou Shalt Be King Thereafter

1947

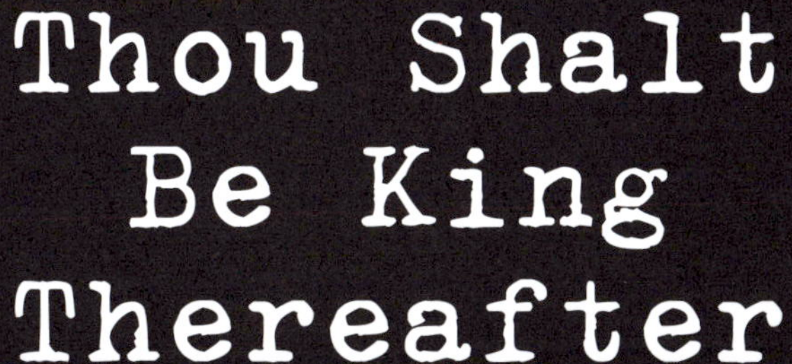

INT. REPUBLIC STUDIOS - NIGHT

Mr. Yates, the head of this studio, was happy enough churning out pulp westerns. Let's not make the man regret one of his rare forays into **CULTURE!**
MACBETH
...Not to mention, I'm on the hook if we run over budget.
That's why we rehearsed like crazy before shooting in this horse-piss-soaked studio.
I want you to act as though you have **BLOOD ON YOUR HANDS...**
But what I want above all is speed...
...AND PACE!
PACE!
PACE!
Daddy?

Yes, Darling Girl?

Orson, you want to check the frame?

Give me a minute, John. It appears I need to **REFRAME** this young lady's expectations...

This movie is important, sweetie. It's maybe the last I'll make here.

So you'll wait for the last shot of the day, like everybody else.
HOLLYWOOD
Oh, I see you're still reading those books about Hollywood, huh?
And about you and your films and...
When I take my own life out of it, and see what they did to other people, I can see that the story of this town is a dirty one.
I'm going to Italy soon. I assume you know where Italy is, Darling Girl?
Well...
Yes, there's a whole world that exists outside of Hollywood. Geography doesn't begin and end with California, you know.
Why are you going to Italy?

I'm going to star in a movie... I'm not directing it. If I want to continue on as an actor, I have to go where there's work...

Soon, nobody in this town is gonna give me a job anymore.
But... **WHY?**

Why?

Because I'm unmanageable.
Profligate.
Unreliable.
That's not true, Dad.
REPUBLIC PICTURES

We had a wonderful time here, Darling Girl, really great while it lasted...
...but it's time for me to move on.

You can go now, sweetie.

Everybody can go, we're done for today.

Hollywood kids!

They have no idea how we make a living in this bloody business.

DAMN IT!

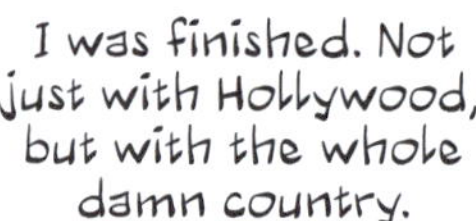

I was finished. Not just with Hollywood, but with the whole damn country.
If I wasn't a pariah before, my inclusion in *Red Channels* cinched it.

To earn an entry in that reactionary little pamphlet was to be effectively **BLACKLISTED.**

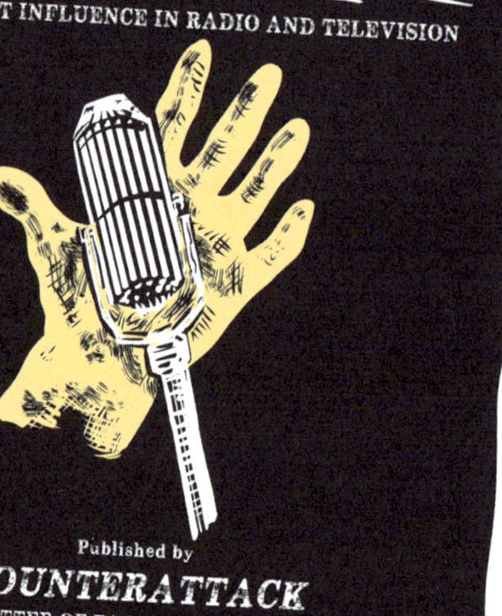
The House Un-American Activities Committee went after me, long before McCarthy started.
Red Channels
COMMUNIST INFLUENCE IN RADIO AND TELEVISION
Published by
COUNTERATTACK
THE NEWSLETTER OF FACTS TO COMBAT COMMUNISM
55 West 42 Street, New York 18, N. Y.
They tried everything to get me...

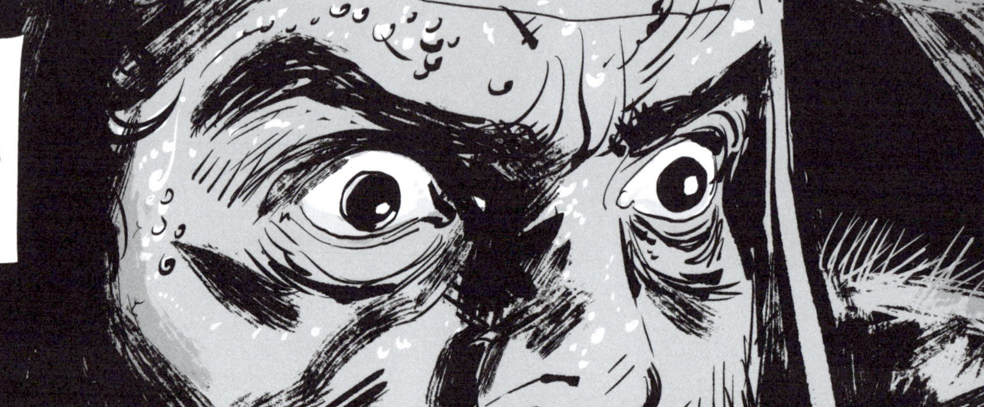
Tax adjustments, harassing my radio partners...even setting shady traps in my hotel rooms...

They would send a few louts over to see me in my office in Hollywood... particularly uneducated and dumb...
Are you a card-carrying communist, Mr. Welles?
Will you first define what a communist is?
What do you mean?
I want to answer your question honestly, that's all...
Just answer the damn question.
A communist believes what they earn should go to the government, right? So here goes:
I'm eighty-six percent communist. The rest is capitalist...
...That's the income tax that one pays in America.
I repeat: Are you a card-carrying communist, Mr. Welles?

Since I was a child, I was told that I would do great things.
CHARLES K. FELDMAN
ORSON
WELLES
MACBETH
JEANETTE NOLAN
I was also told that one day, every spoiled brat gets his comeuppance.

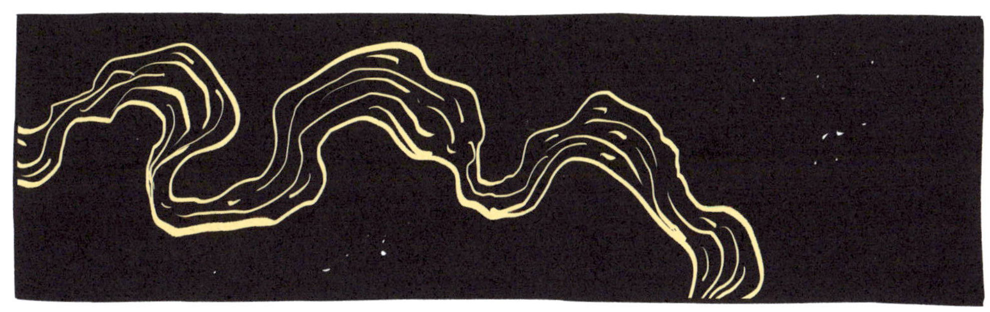

Farewell, Hollywood!

EXT. ESSAOUIRA, MOROCCO - DAY

I like the boldness that you put in your work. And you can do that with an unbelievable economy of means.
ORSON WELLES' magnificent screening of WILLIAM SHAKESPEARE'S immortal tragedy
A story of love and jealousy...
"Othello"
STARRING
ORSON WELLES
SUZANNE CLOUTIER
A MARCEAU FILM PRODUCTION
UNITED ARTISTS

INT. "MA MAISON" RESTAURANT - NIGHT

Remember, Jake has turned into one of those old Hollywood dinosaurs. He's obsessed with the star of his latest movie, this young man who is, in a way, his own dream of himself.
Jake sounds a lot like you, Mr. Welles.

A blackballed director returning to Hollywood to beg for money? Maybe, maybe... But **HE IS NOT** Orson Welles.

By the way, when do you need the funds?

As soon as possible, Mr. Fragoulis.
Yesterday!
MANY YEARS AGO!

Mr. Welles...

I'm Gregor McGill...
Of course you are.
You are a true genius, sir!

I'm either the genius they say I am or the world's godawfulest ham. It's a fifty-fifty split.
MHA HAHAHAHA!

I'm writing a piece about *It's All True*...
Also called: *What Ever Happened in Brazil*...
It's All True wasn't ever true, you know?
Why are you bothering with that? It's ancient history...
It was just a bad script...
It's just that people would love to see that movie, sir.
They probably never will, and that's okay.
And I'm trying to have lunch with my producer here, **CAN'T YOU SEE THAT?**
Sorry, Mr. Welles.
Maybe another time.
Yeah, maybe.
That one's a defunct project. Dead, since 1943...
The whole business literally destroyed my career in Hollywood...

I see here that Astrophore Films has already put a lot of money in the picture...

I'm not asking for much; the movie is almost completed.

Several of my movies as a director have not only been made for nothing but they **COST ME MONEY.**
ساحة أورسن ويلز
PLACE ORSON WELLES

So in a sense, I'm an amateur director...

...in the sense that "amateur" derives from "love."

The Greatest Home Movie Ever Made

1970–1976

EXT. CARFREE, ARIZONA - NIGHT

Wait a sec! Orson, what page are we on?
What the hell difference does it make, John?

Well, I want to know **HOW DRUNK** I'm supposed to be!

Just read the lines, or forget them and say what you please.
The idea is all that matters.

What the fuck is this movie all about?
It's about a bastard director.
It's about us, John.

IT'S ABOUT US.

All right, let's do this.

THE OTHER SIDE OF THE WIND...

...SCENE 103E, TAKE 1!
OTHER WIND
G. GRAVER
SCENE
DATE 3-6-74
TAKE
103E
1

And...

...ACTION!

Remember those Berbers... up in the Atlas?
...They wouldn't let us point a camera at 'em.
EASTMAN
They're certain that it...**DRIES UP** something...
...The old eye, you know, behind the magic box.
Could be it's an evil eye at that... **MEDUSA'S.**
EASTMAN

FIIZ...ZZZ...
KILOWATTHOURS
CL200 240V 3W TYPE J4S 30TA 7.2Kh

FIZZZZZ!

CRACK!

CLIC!
OH, FOR CHRIST'S SAKE!

GARYYYYY!

We're drawing too much juice, and the house's circuit breakers are—
I know, I know! Now, what are you going to do about it?

Don't worry, Orson, I'm on it.

WHO DO I HAVE TO FUCK TO GET OUT OF THIS PICTURE?
I'll have to do another commercial to pay for that.
YOU!
The one with the bunny-in-the-headlights stare.
Go and bring me a big fat generator...
Mr. Welles, it's past midnight, and every store is...
NOW!

GO!

NOW!

WOW!
You scared the shit out of that kid.

You gotta go easy on the crew, Orson. It's a small set.
What can I tell you? We're running out of money.

Again?
We're both horrible with money.
Yup.

Can you believe this? Just as I was returning to sound financial footing, the IRS is hounding me again, after all these years!
Your Swiss production company?
Yeah, now the great state of California's levied a thirty-grand fine for income dating back to 1958.
Ouch!

I have to make a successful box office picture. I'm getting too old not to have made one.

How many features have you completed since we both directed our first films?
Since 1941! Uh... Can't say...

Thirty! Thirty properly produced, big, **REAL MOVIES!**
And here I am, busting my ass to make what's supposed to be my comeback movie... with spit and baling wire.
A home movie.

Big deal.

It's hard to imagine a movie career more littered with sensational catastrophes than mine... and doing business with the Iranians was a nightmare to end all nightmares!

They're on the brink of a revolution.
You can imagine with what interest I watch the damn evening news.

Carefree, Arizona!

This place will sure go down in history.
No, no. It'll go nowhere. This place is for senior citizens who think Ronald Reagan is a communist.

HA!
MHA HAHAHAHAHA!

How could that kid be afraid of me?

Because, Orson, you are a formidable man with a very loud voice, strong opinions, and a wicked sense of humor.

Most people are scared of you.
Me?

I'm just a honey, really! Putty in the right person's hands.

Bullshit...

Dance with Death

1954

INT. ALCÁZAR DE SEGOVIA - NIGHT

NO PRODUCTION HAS GOTTEN ON MY NERVES LIKE THIS ONE!

And do I have to show you how to handle that camera, my friend? I want a low angle, capisce?
I'm... It's the...

Lower...
When I think about the great cameramen I had on *Ambersons* or *The Stranger*...

Lower the damn camera already!
Yes, Mr. Welles...
Go on!

LOWER!
¡VAMOS!
Mr. Arkadin! Take five Bravo, shot thirty-six!
MR. ARKADIN
O.W.
SCENE
5B
SHOT
36
SOUND
And now I'm going to tell you about a scorpion.
This scorpion wanted to cross a river, so he asked the frog to carry him...
ORSON WELLES CONFIDENTIAL REPORT

EXT. MADRID-BARAJAS AIRPORT - DAY

¡Mata lo!
AÑO 1929
PLAZA DE TOROS

You see that?
I can't...

I can't...
I can't
watch.

They have
to do that
to lower the
bull's head,
Darling Girl.

One of my
best friends is
Antonio Ordóñez,
a very famous
matador,
you know.

He would have
loved this bull.

Toledo? How far is it, Daddy?
Not very. There's a beautiful church there with what I consider to be El Greco's greatest work.

So, what do you think of bullfighting, Darling Girl?
I tried hard to like it, but I felt awfully sorry for the bull!

What about the matador? Did you feel sorry for him?

No. He had a sword and could defend himself.
And what if the bull had gored him, sweetie?

How's your mom?
She's all right.

What about school? You like it?
I'm doing okay.

The best way to wreck an original brain is to entrust it to an institution of higher learning.

I liked my time at the Todd School, but that was that.

When I was your age, I had the unwavering will to avoid college at all costs. So I fled to Ireland, hired a donkey cart, and traveled all over the country, painting and sketching.

I found out I wasn't that good of a painter after all! HAHAHAHA!

The windmills, Dad. They're so beautiful.

You should read *Don Quixote* at least once, Darling Girl. It's a great book. One of the greatest. I always wanted to make a movie out of it.

Not anytime soon, honey.
The film crews in Europe don't measure up to the ones in Hollywood, it's true.
But the critics here take me seriously.

Let's say I'm a migratory worker. I go where the jobs are, like a cherry picker.

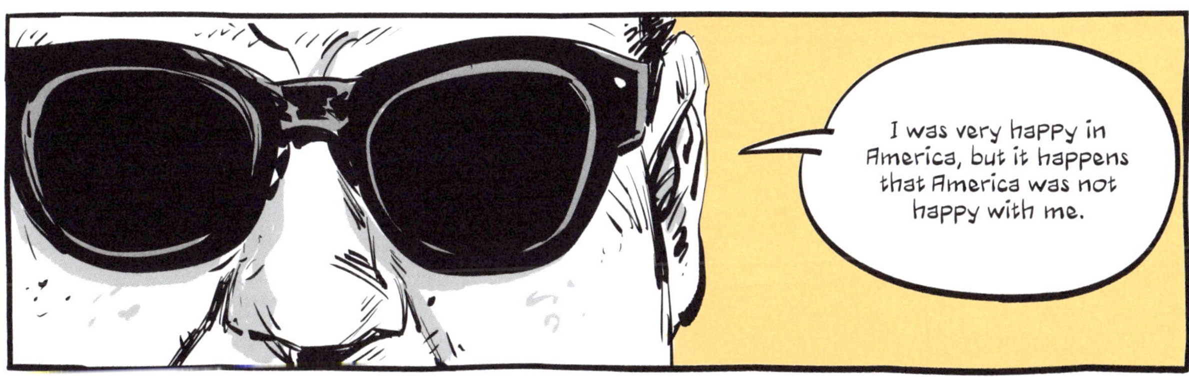
I was very happy in America, but it happens that America was not happy with me.

It started with that unfinished project *It's All True...*

That story about me disappearing in South America is yet another lie, a half-truth at best...and half-truths are ever the darkest of all lies.

It started there, and it's still happening.

They branded me, Darling Girl…
¡TORO!

¡Es un manso!

...To this day, I still feel the red-hot iron EATING through my flesh...
HEY!

The burn
still hurts...

The stigmata still fumes...
¡olé!
¡olé!
¡olé!
¡olé!

HUFF!
HUFF!
HUFF!

¡Estocada!

¡Mata lo!

¡Vamos!

They branded me, all right...
¡Recibiendo!
...THEY BRANDED ME LIKE A CALF.

Grillades
Entrecôte Grillée 7.95
Steak New-York served
with Ma Maison "pommes sautées"

INT. "MA MAISON" RESTAURANT - NIGHT

What? Yeah. Kane, Ambersons... what else?
Wait a second.
WAF! WIF! WOF! WOF! WAF! WAF! WOF!
SHUT UP, KIKI!
Yup, that was Kiki.
GROWL...
The dog's probably as pissed as I am about this whole business. And for good reason!
No! No! The only unfinished work I wanna show is The Other Side!
No Deep, no Quixote!
I hope it's not one of your ideas!
Yes, I'm writing the speech now. I won't improvise, it's simply too important.
This picture is important.
I'm telling you again: no Deep, no Quixote. Those make me look like a cursed artist.
Yes, Peter, thank you.
Bye.
CLAMP!

The Heavy

1957

"Touch of Evil"

BADGE OF EVIL

February 5, 1957

eg #124 - change 10/02/2022

001 INT. STUDIO - NIGHT

MED. SHOT

ORSON WELLES is standing in a dark area of the studio with a lit, half-smoked cigar. He stares straight at the camera defiantly.

WELLES

I'd been in exile in Europe for nearly a decade when Universal decided they wanted me for a film noir. The same sort of police drama they'd been cranking out for thirty-odd years. I was going to play HANK QUINLAN, an almost divinely inspired instrument of justice. To the extent that a policeman's achievement is measured by the number of convictions he is responsible for, Quinlan is something close to a great man.

FRESH ANGLE - TIGHT SHOT

Welles chewing on his cigar, gaze lost in the distant dark sky.

WELLES

But he is also a bully and a bigot, a magnificent scoundrel who commits the most egregious crimes in "the name of the law."

There is no such thing as becoming another character by putting on a lot of makeup. What you're really doing is undressing yourself, and presenting to the public that part of you that corresponds to what you're playing.

There is a villain in each of us, a murderer in each of us, a fascist in each of us, a saint

until my friend Chuck Heston received the script...
Orson is the heavy? I like the sound of that. Why don't you ask him to direct too?
He's a pretty good director, you know.
Oh! Orson as the director, yeah...that's...
Well, that's certainly... um...
We'll, ah, we'll get back to you...
Chuck must have made it clear that we were a package deal. I doubt anyone at Universal was eager to have me back in the director's chair.
All right, let the son of a bitch direct it. How bad can it be?
Heston'll just get sore if we don't let him make it.
Janet Leigh would die to work with him.
Fuckin' actors.
Welles is a loose cannon.
UNIVERSAL PICTURES
COMPANY INC

I had to show them what I could do with this average pulp fiction material. This flick would be an Orson Welles movie.

Well, I might as well write the damn script.

Orson is back in the swim, Janet.

I'll act in any movie by Orson Welles.

And I'd direct it like my independent pictures. It's the only way I know.

Directing is my favorite thing in show business, but it is the most grossly overrated job in the world.

Good paintings don't come from a bad painter, but good motion pictures often come from directors of the most perfect incompetence.

It is not even an art. It is at most an art for a minute a day. This very minute is, of course, absolutely crucial, but much too rare in the course of a day-long shoot.

The notion of directing a film is the invention of critics--the whole eloquence of cinema is achieved in the editing room; it's the only place where one can exercise any control over a film...

This is a Moviola.

It's a machine for editing film, and it's very nearly as important as a camera.
Motion pictures are, at their core, musical.
In the movement from one picture to another is a kind of rhythmic structuring--counterpoint, harmony, and dissonance.

A Moviola is a musical instrument.

I could work forever on the editing of a film. Truffaut says that I shoot as an exhibitionist, and I cut as a censor...
You can toss that one, all right.
It's a shame... It's a nice shot, Mr. Welles.
I know.
But that's what divides the men from the boys... Having the stomach to THROW OUT YOUR MOST BEAUTIFUL SHOTS.
Whatever you say, Mr. Welles.

I wanted to create a nightmare vision, but you can't achieve that through camera tricks alone. You have to speak the language. And the language of film noir was long dead.

Maybe the movie was just too dark and black and strange for them. I'm not sure. There's something missing there that I don't know about, that I'll never understand.

Whatever the case, the producers were getting impatient.

Maybe I had revealed something frightening to them, the same thing that frightened William Randolph Hearst sixteen years earlier.

They felt insulted by the film in a funny way. Hurt and injured, like I'd taken them for some kind of awful ride.

BAR
Muhl is already messing with the cut.

He was happy with the dailies.
I'll make my *Quixote* with **TOTAL FREEDOM,** outside the goddamn system.

Oh, Chuck. You'd be perfect as my Don.

...I just disdain them.

Perhaps because I KNEW they'd take away this movie and mangle it, the same way and for the same reasons they took away *Ambersons*.

Why do they keep doing this to me? I will never know. But there's a shadow, a shadow that broods constantly within me. And when things go wrong, it overtakes me.

It happens whenever I work in this town. It's like somebody who, every time he sticks his nose out, gets struck by lightning.

What I've got is a nose for guilt...

GUILT!

Evidence is for the lawyers.

Maybe everything is my fault.

eg #159 - change 12/6/2022

UNIVERSAL CITY STUDIOS
RETURN TO
CENTRAL FILES

001 INT. BROTHEL - NIGHT

FRESH ANGLE - TIGHT SHOT

Crew is getting on with the scene with MARLENE DIETRICH. Welles is devouring a candy bar. Cameraman setting up the Éclair 35mm.

Ready, honey?

Ready, love.

TANYA
I didn't recognize you.

QUINLAN
Well, it's either the candy or the hooch.
I must say I wish it was your chili
I was getting fat on.

TANYA
You're a mess,
honey.

What did you expect, Marlene?

I couldn't be anything but destroyed by the system.
Here's some news: I've been fired by the studio.
Who'd have thought it, huh?

Now all I need to do is head back to Europe.
They like me there, they like the pictures.

ANTHONY PERKINS

dans

LE PROCÈS

un film de

ORSON WELLES

avec

JEANNE MOREAU

ELSA MARTINELLI

et

ROMY SCHNEIDER

avec

ORSON WELLES

And while I work on my next thing, I'll be spending a lot of time writing memos and trying to salvage *Touch of Evil*. I don't want it to become another mass-market disposable "product."

Orson, we're ready for the last shot.

5¢ Hollywood 1/8 POUND Hollywoo

I love movies, more than ever...

But make no mistake...I hate Hollywood.

Everybody's Shakespeare

1965

EXT. NEAR ÁVILA, SPAIN - DAY

"He wrote it with tears and blood..."

"...and beer, and his words march like heartbeats."

"He speaks to everyone and we all claim him, but it's wise to remember that he doesn't properly belong to us, but to another world..."

"...a florid and entirely remarkable world that smelled of columbine and gunpowder and printer's ink."

All right...
CUT!

GOOD JOB, PEOPLE!
THE BARD HIMSELF WOULD HAVE LOVED THIS BATTLE SCENE!

I hope he would, because we gave it our all.

Normally, this sequence alone would have cost millions.
Money is still a problem. It's always a problem...
Well, filming in black and white should help.

And you know why I like black and white so much, Edmond.
Color enhances the set, the scenery, the costumes, but...
...But it detracts from the actors, right?
ibérico S.A
UNIDAD MOVIL DE RODAJE-CINE-TV

EXACTLY!
Name one outstanding performance by an actor in a color film!
Come on, Orson!

Black and white is what separates the men from the boys because one can't hide behind the **ILLUSION** of reality.

Hell! We were blessed before when we didn't even have **SOUND!** Much easier! No sound to worry about!

Anyway, to make this movie this cheap, I had to cut a bunch of corners...
PRODUCTIO

...and then cut the cuts.
I'm used to it by now.

"Shakespeare speaks everybody's language, but with an Elizabethan accent.

"To know something about Shakespeare, we must know something about that England in which he was born.

"It was a kid of a country, waking up noisily and too suddenly into adolescence and bounding blithely into the sunny, early morning of modern times."

As a child, I myself was woken by Shakespeare —noisily and suddenly— and bounded into theater.

Tragedy!

INT. THE BOAR'S HEAD - NIGHT

Yes, the part is one of a bon vivant, but don't take that at face value.

It takes a bit of experience...

Falstaff is unconcerned with politics. He's content indulging his gargantuan appetite...his appetite for food, for friendship and good cheer, for women. But that's his only flaw.

You know me quite well, chère Jeanne, n'est-ce pas?
I'm trying, Orson.

Traitors are everywhere around us... just like in Shakespeare's tragedies.

Always a Judas lurking somewhere in the shadows of his formidable prose...

...Falstaff is the greatest conception of a good man, the most completely... mmm... good man in all drama. But his goodness is like bread...
...like wine.
People feed off of his goodness, they nourish themselves on it. He lets them take and take, and in the end, of course, he gets nothing in return.

FALSTAFF
My King! My Jove!
I speak to thee,
my heart!

KING
I know thee not, old man.
Fall to thy prayers.
How ill white hairs
become a fool and jester!

I have long dream'd
of such a kind of man,
So surfeit-swell'd,
so old and so profane;

KING
But, being awaked,
I do despise my dream.

And one day, I'll make the ultimate Shakespearian picture...

King Lear...

It's a masterpiece among the masterpieces, because it's truly timeless. It's a story about death and age, and the most terrible ache the elderly must bear: the loss of power.

The strong old man, the leader of the tribe, the city, the church, the state, the political party or corporation...

This man demands love as a tyrant demands tribute...

...and, bereft of power, he must, like Lear, plead for it **LIKE A BEGGAR.**

CLING!
Let's drink to Shakespeare!

To his jesters and kings!
MHA HAHAHAHA!

To me, you're a king, Orson.
A beautiful, destitute king...

Not because you were thrown away from the kingdom, but because on this earth, the way the world is...
Aouch!

...there is no kingdom good enough for Orson Welles.
Careful with my nose, Jeanne!
Orson Welles
FALSTAFF
Margaret Rutherford
Jeanne Moreau

If sack and sugar
be a fault,
God help the wicked!
If to be old and merry
be a sin, then many
an old host that
I know is damned.

UNIUS J.
ANNAFORD

ORSON WELLES
F for Fake
starring Orson Welles
Oja Kodar
Elmyr de Hory
Clifford Irving
Francois Reichen

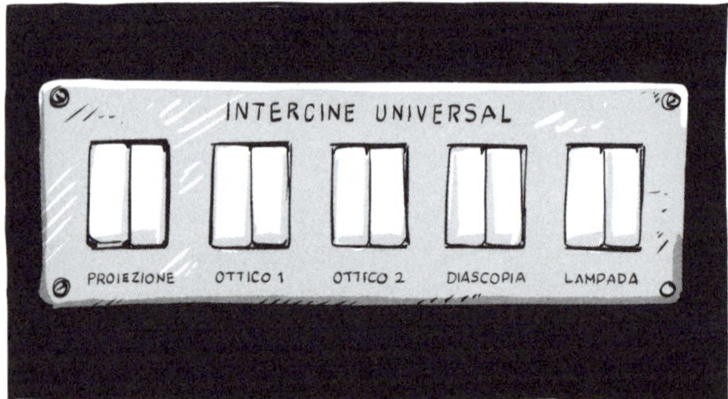
INTERCINE UNIVERSAL
PROIEZIONE
OTTICO 1
OTTICO 2
DIASCOPIA
LAMPADA

TIC!

OTHER WIND
G. GRAVER
DATE
74
SCENE
TAKE
183E
3

SHOT MISSING

Listen, kid.
Listen...

And if to be fat
be to be hated,
then Pharaoh's
lean kine are
to be loved.

No, my good lord; banish Peto,
banish Bardolph, banish Poins:
but for sweet Jack Falstaff,
kind Jack Falstaff,
true Jack Falstaff,
valiant Jack Falstaff,
and therefore more valiant,
being, as he is, old Jack Falstaff,

banish not him
thy Harry's company,
banish not him
thy Harry's company:
banish plump Jack,
and banish all the world.

CLIC!
...shington, the president and the shah met for about an hour this morning...

The president said the shah's visit was encouraging and had strengthened the strong ties of friendship between the two countries...

...despite the temporary imposition of martial law, the shah's new government appears determined to press ahead with liberal reform...

MUNCH MUNCH
...the number killed in Tehran at the beginning of the month is probably well over a hundred...
MUNCH MUNCH

CHOMP CHAMP
CHOMP CHAMP

...but people in this crowd were saying and believing seven thousand had been killed...
GORGL GORGL GORG!

...almost forty thousand refinery workers went on strike today, virtually cutting off Iran's petroleum exports...
BURRRPA!

University students demonstrating in Tehran, shouting "death to the shah," pledge allegiance to the movement of the ayatollahs...
DEATH TO THE SHAH!
DEATH TO THE SHAH!
DEATH TO THE SHAH!

DEATH TO THE SHAH!

DEATH TO THE SHAH!

DEATH TO THE SHAH!

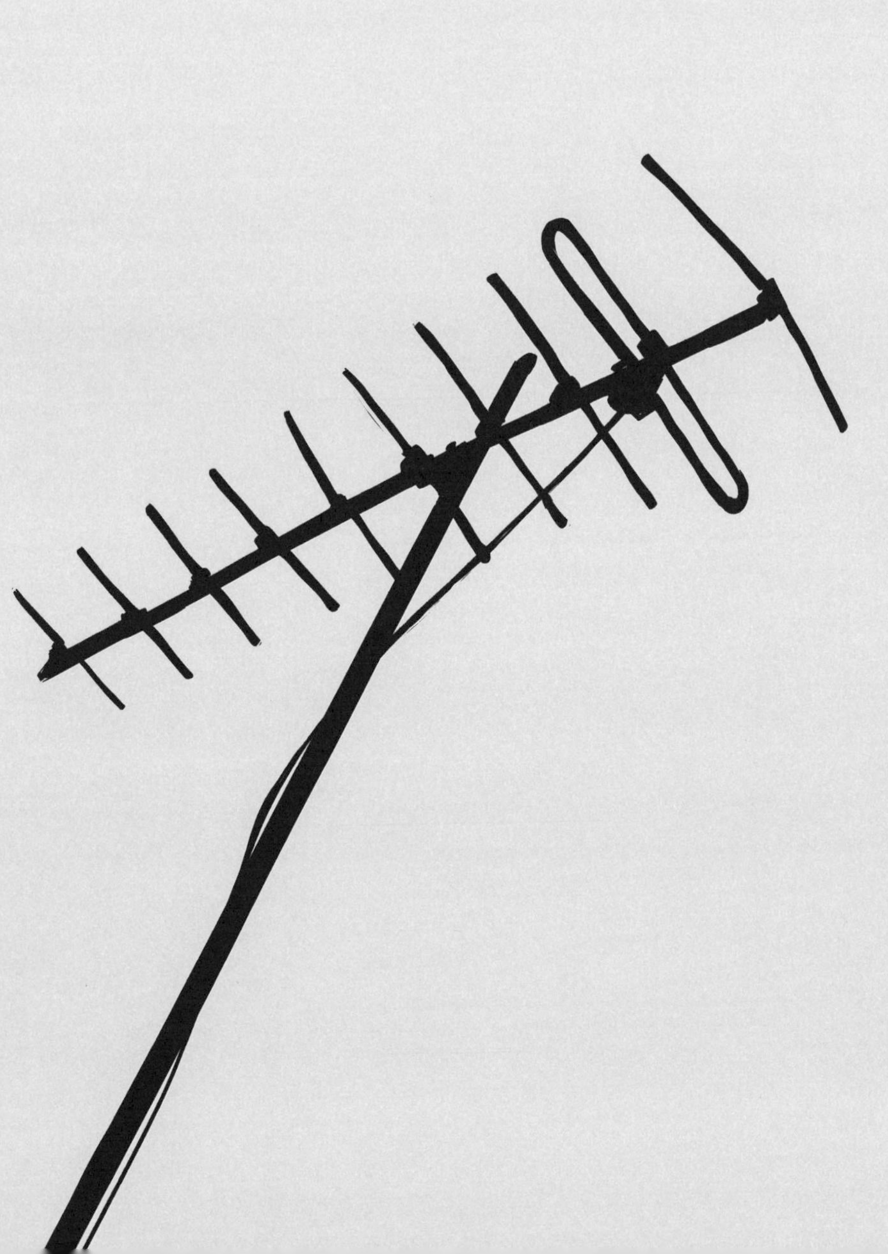

The Dancing Bear

1975

Hello, I'm Orson Welles...

It was Shakespeare who said, "Things won are done... joy's soul lies in the doing."

...some things can't be rushed: good music and good wine...
...It's like magic, but there's no magic involved here...
...when you buy a Kimoto copier, you're also buying cutting-edge laser copy technology...
Hello, I'm Orson Welles.
I direct films, and my goal is to make a flawless picture...
...in my trade, that's only a wish...
...but with Y&D Scotch, you sure have it... flawlessness!
Shakespeare said that "we know what we are but know not what we may be."
...A great deal of time and care go into the production of a fine play, just as they go into the making of a fine wine.
KIMO

This incredible board game transported me to another world...
Your number one choice!
The best money can buy!
This is what whiskey is all about.
If you want sharp pictures, this has got to be your camera...
"How far that little candle throws his beams!" Well, Shakespeare would have said that if he'd seen this fine piece of engineering...
Now you don't have to wait years for pay-per-view TV...
The bourbon that's been enchanting us for more than a century...
Never has a beer been better than this!
AAAAAH! The French Champagne!
The taste of French champagne has always been celebrated for its excellence...

In fact, this **IS** all you're doing nowadays...

WHORING!

AAAAAH!
The French
Champagne!
AIRLINES
Kimoto

AHAAAAAH!

The French Champagne!

AAAAAAH! The French Champagne!

MHAAAA! The French Champagne!

AAAAAH! The French Champagne!

INT. "MA MAISON" RESTAURANT

All right, I see that you still need to pay for the camera rentals...
My goodness! How many cameras are you guys using?
All right! The catering bill is absolutely huge! Oh!
Blah blah blah blah blah blah blah blah blah blah blah blah blah blah blah blah blah blah...
Okay, thirty-five thousand plus fifty-nine... There's something I don't understand...
Blah blah blah blah blah blah a couple grand here, a couple grand there... Blah blah blah...
Blah blah blah blah blah blah blah blah blah blah blah blah blah blah blah blah blah blah...
You're relaxed...
Oh, and there's something I don't get with the Iranian issue, the money is blah blah blah...
I beg your pardon?

Now you are **AWARE!**

You know that this may be **THE MOST IMPORTANT MOVIE OF MY CAREER...**

Don't think...

Just do **AS I SAY...**

GIVE ME THE
MONEEEY!

INT. CENTURY PLAZA HOTEL - NIGHT

My father once told me that the art of receiving a compliment is of all things the sign of a civilized man.

AFI

This honor I can only accept in the name of all the mavericks.

A maverick may go his own way, but he doesn't think that it's the only way or ever claim that it's the best one... except maybe for himself.
AFI
ORSON WELLES 1975

It's just that some of the necessities to which I am a slave are different from yours.

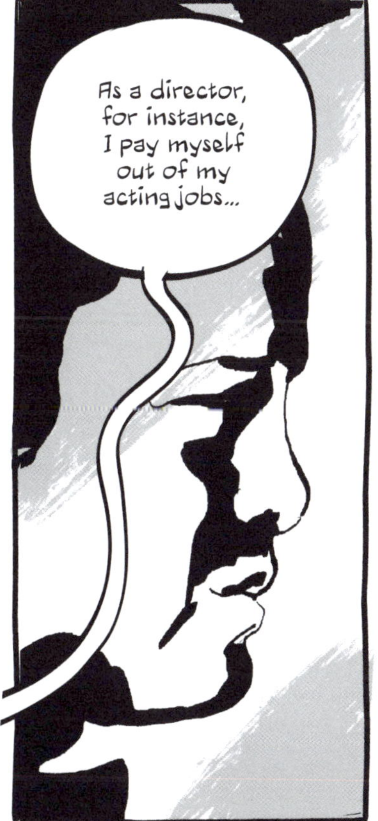
As a director, for instance, I pay myself out of my acting jobs...

...I use my own work to subsidize my work. In other words...

...I'm crazy.

Good evening, I'm Orson Welles.
Are you familiar with lobby cards?

Their purpose is to incite your curiosity, to whet your appetite, to **HYPNOTIZE YOU** into buying a ticket...
You know, the ones they put in the theater lobby...

That's the magic of cinema!
Now, pick a card, any card...

Nobody in the world has acted in worse films than I.
PRINCE OF FOXES
TYRONE POWER · ORSON WELLES · WANDA HENDRIX
ORSON WELLES MERCURY PRODUCTION
JOURNEY INTO FEAR
JOSEPH COTTEN · DOLORES DEL RIO · RUTH WARRICK
ORSON WELLES
Copyright 1942 RKO Radio Pictures Inc. Country of Origin U.S.A.
ORSON WELLES
NANCY GUILD
AKIM TAMIROFF
VALENTINA CORTESE
FRANK LATIMORE
MARGOT GRAHAME
BLACK MAGIC
THE BIGGEST PICTURE IN TEN YEARS!
They hire me when they have a really bad movie and they want a cameo that will give it a little class.
nte a Roma
più atteso!
ORSON WELLES
VIVIANE ROMANCE
BESTIA e la VIRTU
TROUBLE IN THE GLEN
INTERNATIONAL PICTURES presents
Claudette Colbert Orson Welles George Brent
TOMORROW IS FOREVER
ARGUMENTO Y GUION: GRAHAM GREENE
The Black Rose
Color by TECHNICOLOR
TYRONE POWER ORSON WELLES
I'm often asked: "Why did you do this one?"
For the money...
What a silly question!

This one? I did it for the tamales.
20th
JERRY WALD'S production of WILLIAM FAULKNER'S
The Long, Hot Summer
PAUL NEWMAN - JOANNE WOODWARD - ANTHONY FRANCIOSA - ORSON WELLES
COLOR BY DE LUXE
CINEMASCOPE
Directed by MARTIN RITT
Screenplay by IRVING RAVETCH and HARRIET FRANK Jr
This one? For the bacon, of course.
STARRING
ORSON WELLES
JOHN GREGSON
ELIZABETH SELLARS
"THREE CASES OF MURDER"
The cabbage!
The firebrand who helped forge a nation... with his courage... and his sword!
JACK HAWKINS
VITTORIO DE SICA
PASCALE AUDRET
KAMPF UM ROM
1. TEIL
Gimme the cheese, thank you, sir.
The bread.

Listen, I needed the smackeroonies, you understand?
Give me a break, I did this one for the moola too. I look like Werner Krauss in *The Cabinet of Dr. Caligari*!
GEORGE PEPPARD INGER STEVENS ORSON WELLES
"HOUSE OF CARDS"
TECHNICOLOR
KEITH MICHELL
SI VERSAILLES M'ÉTAIT CONTÉ
C.L.M.
CRACK IN THE MIRROR
CINEMASCOPE
ORSON WELLES · JULIETTE GRECO · BRADFORD DILLMAN
DARRYL F. ZANUCK · RICHARD FLEISCHER · MARK CANFIELD · MARCEL HAEDRICH
DARRYL F. ZANUCK'S
THE ROOTS OF HEAVEN
JOHN HUSTON
The dough, ladies and gentlemen.
JEFF CHANDLER · ORSON WELLES · COLLEEN MILLER
"MAN IN THE SHADOW"
This one I did for the scratch, but it was one of those things that happens to a man when he finds himself in the wrong country and stuck on the wrong girl.
The only thing I want written on my tombstone: "He never did *Love Boat*."

Stinkers, z-movies, big-budget schlock, I did it all. I used so many nasal prosthetics, I ran out of hooters.
CATCH-22
COLUMBIA PICTURES presents
FRED ZINNEMANN'S FILM OF
A MAN FOR ALL SEASONS
From the play by ROBERT BOLT
WENDY HILLER · LEO McKERN · ROBERT SHAW
ORSON WELLES · SUSANNAH YORK
PAUL SCOFIELD
M.G.M presents
A WX FILM Production
'THE TARTARS'
ALL NEW!
NEVER BEFORE SEEN ON ANY SCREEN!
ORSON WELLES
DAVID AND GOLIATH
TOTALSCOPE
And I took work wherever there was work, until I ran out of countries.

LE MARIN DE GIBRALTAR
ORSON WELLES · TOMAS MILIAN
TEPEPA
THERE IS NO EQUAL TO THIS CHRONICLE OF RAW COURAGE AND STUBBORN SAVAGERY!
BATTLE of NERETVA
YUL BRYNNER · SERGEI BONDARCUK
CURT JURGENS · SILVA KOSCINA
HARDY KRUGER · FRANCO NERO · ORSON WELLES
A small nose like mine is pleasant enough for everyday use... but for dramatic purposes, I detest it. Better a false nose than a button one.
CURT JURGENS · ORSON WELLES · SYLVIA SYMS
A LEWIS GILBERT PRODUCTION
FERRY to HONG KONG
SPENSER
CINEMASCOPE COLOR by DE LUXE
ORSON WELLES MARLENE JOBERT MICHEL PICCOLI ANTHONY PERKINS
LA DECADE PRODIGIEUSE
Brando used heavy makeup as well, when he played Don Corleone.
I would have sold my soul to have been in *The Godfather*, only those "New Hollywood" bearded hipsters kept ignoring me.
Ungrateful suckers!

I would have been more successful if I'd left movies immediately, stayed in the theater, gone into politics, written—anything.
TONY CURTIS ORSON WELLES & ERIK ESTRADA
Donald Pleasence Ron Moody
Cassandra Domenica Peter Lawford
Where is Parsifal?
I had to keep myself independent, but no amount of money is worth the hassle.
PARIS BRÛLE-T-IL ?
CHARLES K. FELDMAN
CASINO ROYALE
PETER SELLERS
URSULA ANDRESS
DAVID NIVEN
WOODY ALLEN
JOANNA PETTET
ORSON WELLES
DALIAH LAVI
DEBORAH KERR
WILLIAM HOLDEN
CHARLES BOYER
JEAN PAUL BELMONDO
GEORGE RAFT
JOHN HUSTON
TERENCE COOPER
BARBARA BOUCHET
GABRIELLA LICUDI
TRACY REED
TRACEY CRISP
KURT KASZNAR
ELAINE TAYLOR
ANGELA SCOULAR
plus a Bondwagon full of the most beautiful and talented girls you ever saw!
JAMES BOND 007
CASINO ROYALE
CHARLES K. FELDMA
CASIN
ROYA
IS TOO
FO
JAM
THE BATTLE THAT CHANGED THE FACE OF THE WORLD.
WATERLOO

NOW ORSON WELLES as "Long John Silver."
TREASURE ISLAND
ORSON WELLES
Tom Smothers John Astin Katharine Ross—Orson
Get to know your Rabbit
ORSON WELLES
MALPERTUIS
MICHEL BOUQUET MATHIEU CARRIERE
JEAN-PIERRE CASSEL
HARRY KUMEL
J. SANTOS
United Artists
The silly talk shows and the sillier ads.
I've spent too much energy on things that have nothing to do with making movies.
My movies, with my stories, my writing, my editing.
It's been two percent moviemaking and ninety-eight percent HUSTLING.
It's no way to spend a life.

Let us raise our cups and drink together to what really matters to us all, to our crazy and beloved profession.
To the movies! **TO GOOD MOVIES, TO EVERY POSSIBLE KIND.**
I leave you now with another very short scene from my upcoming film, still in the works, ***THE OTHER SIDE OF THE WIND...***

Do they still love you?
CLAP CLAP CLAP CLAP CLAP CLAP

Why Orson Welles? He's only made one movie.
The son of a bitch doesn't deserve it.
Well, he might have **SOME** friends left in Hollywood...
Orson has no friends, only stooges.
He wants us to give him money? To fund his film, is that right?
Looks like it.

Not a chance.

EXT. CAREFREE, ARIZONA - NIGHT

JAKE
Who knows? Maybe you can stare too hard at something, huh? Drain out the virtue, suck out the living juice.
You shoot the great places and the pretty people, all those girls and boys-- shoot 'em dead.

PAW!

PAW!

CLAC
PAW!

CLAC
PAW!
GO ON, JOHN!

WHACK 'EM!
CLAC

KAPOW!

WHACK 'EM ALL!
PAW!

PAW!

You know, Orson, I'm still trying to wrap my head around the plot...

Who needs a plot, Ed? What you have here is a good story...

PAW!

Good stories... Like we used to make 'em in Hollywood.

Ah, what happened to those times when we'd make movies and fuck all night?

KAPOW!

Forget about the detritus of the Golden Age, Edmond. We're living in the Fool's Gold Era...

...EASY RIDER'S ERA.
PAW!

HOLLYWOOD

HOLLY

MELROSE AVE.
→7600 W.
Rosebud
VIDEO

INT. "MA MAISON" RESTAURANT - NIGHT

How many times I've pictured that scene with Huston saying: "Listen, kid, listen..."
This is my best story.
It touches a nerve with you, doesn't it?
Oh yes!
You're not recording, are you?
Nope. Out of tape.
Oh, thank God!
Well, I'm a complete fool!
I thought they would line up and beg me to take their money.
SIDE 1
HIGH FIDELITY
Eat a little shit, Orson.
Wake up, Kiki! Let's go.

I have a sudden urge to write a few pages tonight.
I understand.

PICARD
PICAR
Good night, Peter.
Night, Orson.

You know, there's something about writing I always find very hard, Peter.
What's that?
It's that terrible silence when you wind up a chapter...

...and the damn typewriter doesn't **BURST INTO APPLAUSE.**

MHA HAHAHAHA!
Good night, Orson.
Night, Mr. Welles.
Good night, Patrick.
See you tomorrow.
Ma Maison
PICARD
PICARD

All right, you want to stretch your little legs?
FLIP DISCOUNT WAREHOUSE
FLIP

You behave yourself. Promise?

I have to **THINK!**

FLASH FOOT MELROSE
MESA GEAR

MUAAAHA HAHAHAHAHA!

WHO KNOWS WHAT EVIL LURKS IN THE HEARTS OF MEN?

THE SHADOW KNOWS! MUAHA HAHA!

INT. THE STAGE - NIGHT
Well, I'll be damned...
So...?
...How's that big comeback going?
What do you mean?

I mean the goddamn movie you've been making for years now...
...THE OTHER SIDE OF THE WIND...
...IT ISN'T FINISHED YET, IS IT?
It's coming along just fine.
I'll pull it off, just like I always do.
What on earth is this place?

"You'll pull it off"... You mean like you did with *Quixote*?

AY! You may be able to ask him yourself, master. He's right there!
WHAT?

ORSON!

Dios mio, Orson, where have you been?
What's the end of the story?
Hey, Orson! The atomic explosion! When are we going to see it?

We've been wandering for years without you.
Lo siento, querido Francisco.

I begged you to finish the movie **BEFORE I DIE!**

You look great in the dailies, Akim, my old friend.
Keep moving, guys...

...That's what a knight errant and his squire are supposed to do.

The fear of completion... might be a thing, this... syndrome they're talking about...
Come on now! It's happened too often for it to be entirely **ACCIDENTAL.**
Spare me your dollar-book Freud bullshit.
Quixote is a private exercise of mine... and it's not unfinished because of financial reasons. It will be finished as an author would finish it: in my own good time, **WHEN I FEEL LIKE IT...**
TESTO
DREAMERS
THE DEEP
QUIXOTE
All right. What about all the other unfinished stuff? *The Deep, The Dreamers...* Can't remember them all...
BAD LUCK! How do you like that?

I had the worst bad luck in the history of cinema, but that's in the order of things: I had to pay for having had the best luck in the history of cinema.
Luck had nothing to do with it. It took **A GENIUS** to churn out a friggin' masterpiece at only twenty-five!
I've been called a genius since I was in diapers. It never occurred to me that I wasn't one until middle age.
HA!
HOLLY

I'm everything an artist shouldn't be: uncommercial and unconventional.
Yes, and without the business sense to make up for it. Too busy making obtuse films for an ever-shrinking audience. Maybe you were too far ahead of your time.
Well, Hollywood doesn't like that, you see?
They like people who are *barely* ahead of their time, like a **FEW SECONDS** ahead. Those are the ones who make money.

Stop lamenting your fate, you're okay.

I'm awfully tired of old men saying they have no regrets.

You know what? **I DO HAVE REGRETS,** Mr. Shadow!

We're LOADED with regrets...
Don't...
...BURDENED with regrets...
Stop...
...We're FALLING UNDER the weight of regrets.
I said...
STOP!

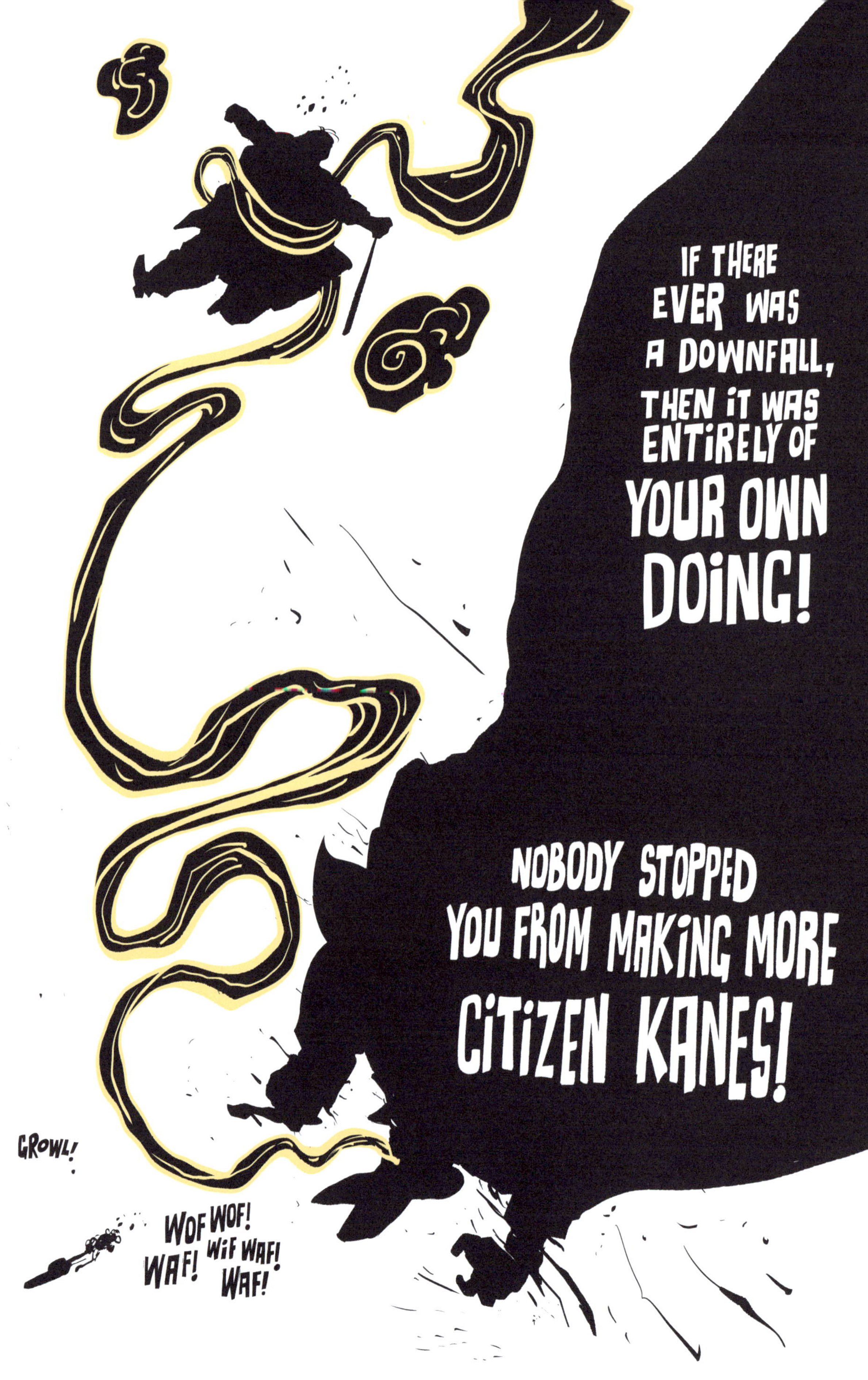
IF THERE EVER WAS A DOWNFALL, THEN IT WAS ENTIRELY OF YOUR OWN DOING!
NOBODY STOPPED YOU FROM MAKING MORE CITIZEN KANES!
GROWL!
WOF WOF! WAF! WIF WAF! WAF!

QUIXOTE

All right.
Gimme some light here.

Zoom in a bit.
Enough.
That's perfect there.

No.

Nobody stopped me from doing anything.

Nobody could.
MITCHELL

My love for the movies is stronger than they could ever imagine.

I'm going to keep working from the terribly expensive paint box that is film.
And I'll keep trying new things.
There is still room for innovation in storytelling...
...and filming...
...and editing...
Pictures are becoming more... adventurous. The opportunities ahead of me are greater, much greater than they were a few years ago.

Fzzzzzzzz
I never lost that appetite...
...that HUNGER!

All right...
And now, I'm going home. I have no more time for your charades.
What's the way out of this dump?
This way...
Over that hill...

...and this is a goddamn stage, all right? **A STAGE!**
Whatever you say.

Just
promise me this:
Finish the film.

Oh yes...
I will finish *The Other Side*...

You bet your
sweet life
I will.

DAOUDI '23

I'm
Orson Welles.
ORSON WELL

ESLAND

If you want a
happy ending, that
depends, of course,
on where you stop
your story.

George Orson Welles
1915-1985

2 3 4 5 6 7 8 9 0
Q W E R T Y U I O P
A S D F G H J K L
SHIFT KEY
Z X C V B N M
SHIFT KEY

A graphic novel about Orson Welles?

There have been numerous books written about Orson Welles, but graphic novels exploring his story are relatively scarce. Even if all the books in the world attempted to capture the complexity, contradictions, and paradoxes of such an extraordinary individual, a graphic novel would fall even shorter. However, since my first venture into this medium, I have been continually fascinated by the limitless narrative tools it offers. I was certain that Orson Welles himself, a giant of cinema, theater, and radio, would feel right at home within its pages.

Welles's journey was anything but smooth sailing. His life and career were unlike any other artist of his time. Many believe that he did not receive the full recognition he deserved for his work. Yet there are also those who argue that his career and level of success, or lack thereof, were exactly what he deserved.

I had to dig deep researching everything about Welles; it took me years to read, annotate, and arrange the thousands of pages that this extraordinary man generated while he lived and for many years after he left the world of the living. I had to understand him, draw him in every way possible, and sculpt his face hoping to decipher his profound mystery.

Nevertheless, when endeavoring to create a portrait, it invariably becomes a manifestation of the artist's personal viewpoint.

The subject becomes the artist's reflection in an idealized mirror. This book is not solely about Orson Welles. In fact, Welles serves as a captivating pretext to explore something perhaps greater than the immense persona he embodied: the profound journey of a true artist.

Youssef Daoudi

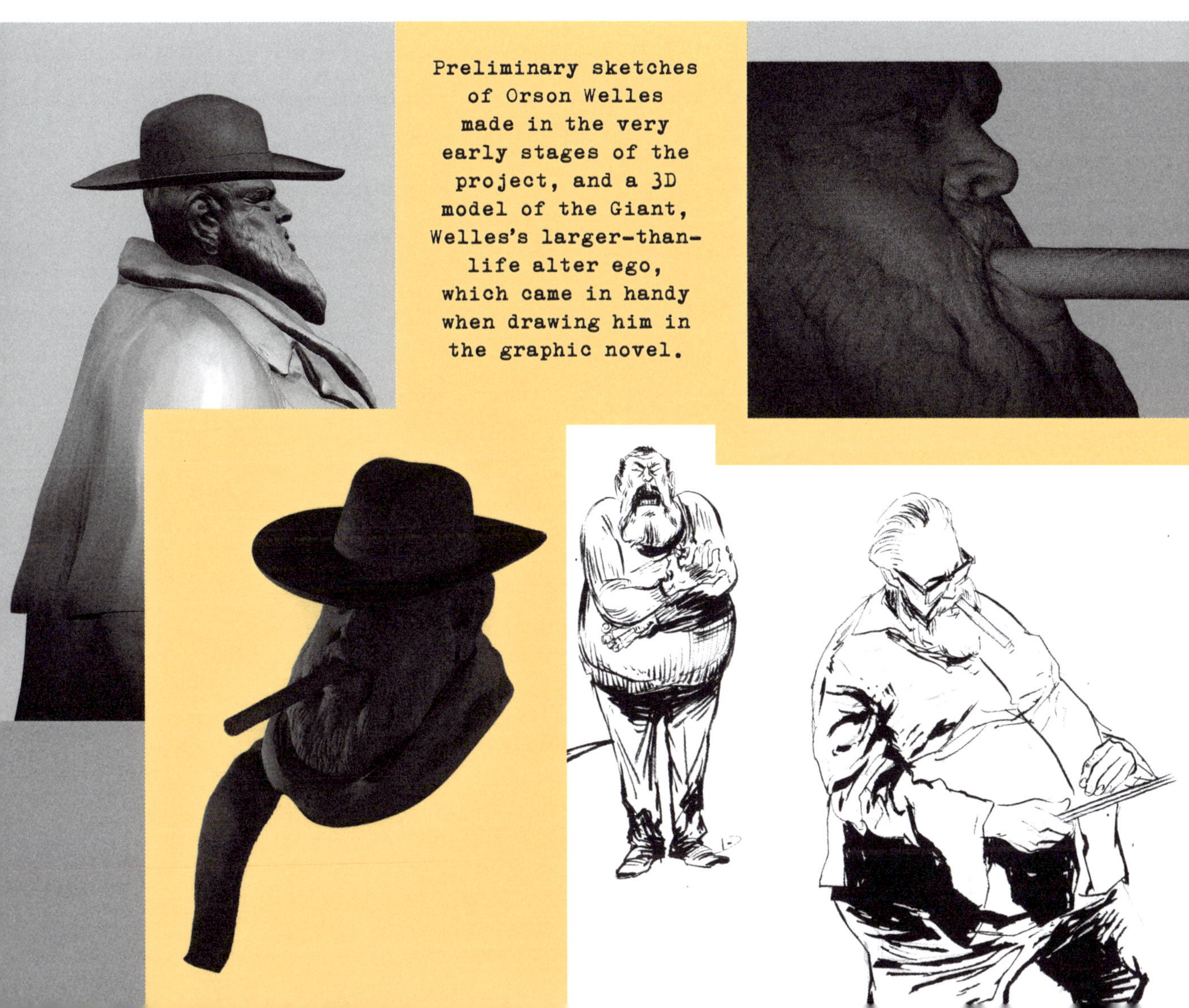

Preliminary sketches of Orson Welles made in the very early stages of the project, and a 3D model of the Giant, Welles's larger-than-life alter ego, which came in handy when drawing him in the graphic novel.

Telling Welles's story wouldn't have been possible without digging deep into a huge body of existing research. Much of the text quotes Orson Welles and some of the people that were close to him. I want to thank all of them, the living and the dead: Christopher Welles Feder, Peter Bogdanovich, John Houseman, John Huston, Jeanne Moreau, and Charlton Heston. I also want to express my gratitude and admiration for all the biographers, writers, journalists, and filmmakers whose keen observations of Welles and careful documentation have given us such a detailed record of his words.

Bibliography

Bazin, André. *Orson Welles*. Paris: Cahiers du Cinéma, 1998.

Benamou, Catherine L. *It's All True: Orson Welles's Pan-American Odyssey*. Berkeley and Los Angeles, CA: University of California Press, 2007.

Berthomé, Jean-Pierre, and François Thomas. *Orson Welles at Work*. Translated by Imogen Forster, Roger Leverdier, and Trista Selous. New York: Phaidon Press, 2008.

Brady, Frank. *Citizen Welles: A Biography of Orson Welles*. New York: Charles Scribner's Sons, 1989.

Feeney, F. X. *Welles*. Movie Icons, edited by Paul Duncan. Cologne, Germany: Taschen, 2006.

Heston, Charlton. *In the Arena: An Autobiography*. New York: Simon & Schuster, 1995.

Heylin, Clinton. *Despite the System: Orson Welles Versus the Hollywood Studios*. Chicago: Chicago Review Press, 2005.

Jaglom, Henry, and Orson Welles. *My Lunches with Orson: Conversations between Henry Jaglom and Orson Welles*. Edited by Peter Biskind. New York: Metropolitan Books, 2013.

Karp, Josh. *Orson Welles's Last Movie: The Making of "The Other Side of the Wind."* New York: St. Martin's Press, 2015.

McBride, Joseph. *What Ever Happened to Orson Welles? A Portrait of an Independent Career*. Lexington, KY: University Press of Kentucky, 2006.

Naremore, James. *The Magic World of Orson Welles*. 3rd ed. Champaign, IL: University of Illinois Press, 2015. First published 1978 by Oxford University Press.

Shakespeare, William, Orson Welles, and Roger Hill. *Everybody's Shakespeare*. Woodstock, IL: The Todd Press, 1934.

Welles, Orson, and Peter Bogdanovich. *This Is Orson Welles: Orson Welles and Peter Bogdanovich*. Edited by Jonathan Rosenbaum. New York: Da Capo Press, 1998.

Welles Feder, Chris. *In My Father's Shadow: A Daughter Remembers Orson Welles*. New York: Algonquin Books, 2009.

Articles & Websites

Brody, Richard. "Herman Mankiewicz, Pauline Kael, and the Battle over Citizen Kane." *New Yorker*, November 14, 2020.

Leaming, Barbara. "Orson Welles: The Unfulfilled Promise." *New York Times*, July 14, 1985.

Welles, Orson. "But Where Are We Going?" *Look*, November 3, 1970.

Welles, Orson. "Interview with Orson Welles." By André Bazin and Charles Bitsch. *Cahiers du Cinéma*, no. 84, June 1958. Translated and annotated by Sally Shafto, *Senses of Cinema*, no. 46, March 2008.

Welles, Orson. Letter to the editor. *New Statesman*, May 24, 1958.

Welles, Orson. "Twilight in the Smog." *Esquire*, March 1, 1959.

Welles, Orson. "Welles on Falstaff: Interview with Orson Welles." By Juan Cobos and Miguel Rubio. *Cahiers du Cinéma*, no. 179, June 1966.

wellesnet.com

themagnificentambersons.com

Documentaries

Cousins, Mark, dir. *The Eyes of Orson Welles*. Bridge of Allan, UK: Bofa Productions, 2018.

Kapnist, Élisabeth, dir. *Orson Welles: Autopsie d'une legende* (Orson Welles: Shadows & Light). Paris: CPB Films, 2015.

Maysles, Albert, and David Maysles, dirs. *Orson Welles in Spain*. Documentary short. New York: Maysles Films, 1963.

Megahey, Leslie, and Alan Yentob, dirs. *Arena: The Orson Welles Story*. BBC, 1982.

Neville, Morgan, dir. *They'll Love Me When I'm Dead*. Los Gatos, CA: Netflix, 2018.

Reichenbach, François, and Frédéric Rossif, dirs. *Portrait: Orson Welles*. Documentary short. France: Le Capricorne, 1968.

Stevens, George, Jr., and Paul Keyes, prods. *AFI Life Achievement Award: A Tribute to Orson Welles*. Aired February 17, 1975, on CBS.

Welles, Orson, dir. *Around the World with Orson Welles*. Documentary series. Aired October 7 to December 16, 1955, on ITV.

Welles, Orson, dir. *Filming "Othello."* Germany: Hellwig Productions, 1978.

Welles, Orson, dir. *Filming "The Trial."* Unfinished. Filmed November 14, 1981. Available in the public domain.

Welles, Orson, dir. *One Man Band* (a.k.a. *Orson Welles' London*). Unfinished. Filmed 1968-1971. Aired July 10, 2001, on Arte.

Welles, Orson, dir. *Orson Welles' Magic Show*. Unfinished and unaired documentary series. Filmed 1976-1985. Available in the public domain.

Welles, Orson, dir. *Orson Welles' Sketch Book*. Documentary series. Aired April 24 to July 3, 1955, on the BBC.

Welles, Orson. *Parkinson*. Interview by Michael Parkinson. Aired November 17, 1973, on the BBC.

Wilson, Richard, Myron Meisel, and Bill Krohn, dirs. *It's All True: Based on an Unfinished Film by Orson Welles*. Los Angeles: Paramount Pictures, 1993.

Workman, Chuck, dir. *Magician: The Astonishing Life and Work of Orson Welles*. New York: Cohen Media Group, 2014.

I want to thank my friend Igor Olafs, a fervent Welles enthusiast whose conversations were instrumental in navigating the complexities of the project. Many thanks to my agent, my editor, and the entire team that made this book possible. I'm especially grateful to my wife, my beloved and guiding light, whose unwavering support sustained me during the many moments of sheer exhaustion and doubt.

Filmography (director)

1941: *Citizen Kane*

1942: *The Magnificent Ambersons*

1946: *The Stranger*

1947: *The Lady from Shanghai*

1948: *Macbeth*

1951: *Othello*

1955: *Mr. Arkadin* (a.k.a. *Confidential Report*)

1958: *Touch of Evil*

1962: *The Trial* (a.k.a. *Le procès*)

1966: *Chimes at Midnight* (a.k.a. *Campanadas a medianoche*)

1968: *The Immortal Story* (a.k.a. *Une histoire immortelle*)

1973: *F for Fake* (a.k.a. *Vérités et mensonges*)

1977: *Filming "Othello"*

2018: *The Other Side of the Wind* (posthumously completed and released by Netflix)

Filmography (unfinished)

1941–1943: *It's All True*

1955–1985: *Don Quixote*

1966–1973: *The Deep*

1967: *The Heroine*

1968–1971: *Orson's Bag*

1969–1985: *The Magic Show*

1970–1985: *The Other Side of the Wind*

1971: *Moby Dick*

1978–1982: *The Dreamers*

1981: *Filming "The Trial"*

1985: *King Lear*

Theater credits (non-exhaustive)

1918: "Trouble" in *Madama Butterfly* by Giacomo Puccini, Luigi Illica, and Giuseppe Giacosa – dir. Cleofonte Campanini – Chicago Opera Company – Ravinia Opera House, Chicago

1927: "Mary" in a nativity play – dir. Roger Hill – Todd Seminary for Boys, Woodstock, IL

1930: "Ferrovius" in *Androcles and the Lion* by George Bernard Shaw, adapt. Orson Welles – dir. Orson Welles – Todd Troupers – Woodstock Women's Club, Woodstock, IL

1931: "Duke Karl Alexander of Württemberg" in *Jew Süss* by Ashley Dukes, adapt. from the novel by Lion Feuchtwanger – dir. Hilton Edwards – Dublin Gate Theatre Company – Gate Theatre, Dublin

1932: *The Lady from the Sea* by Henrik Ibsen – dir. Orson Welles – unknown theater, Dublin

1933–1934: "Mercutio" in *Romeo and Juliet* by William Shakespeare – dir. Guthrie McClintic – Katharine Cornell's repertory company – US tour

1934: "McGafferty" in *Panic* by Archibald MacLeish – dir. James Light – John Houseman's Phoenix Theatre Group – Imperial Theatre, New York

1936: *Macbeth* by William Shakespeare, adapt. Orson Welles - dir. Orson Welles - Federal Theatre Project (FTP) - Lafayette Theatre, New York

1936: "Mugglethorpe" in *Horse Eats Hat* by Edwin Denby and Orson Welles, adapt. from *The Italian Straw Hat* by Eugène Labiche and Marc-Michel - dir. Orson Welles - FTP - Maxine Elliott's Theatre, New York

1937: "Faustus" in *The Tragical History of Doctor Faustus* by Christopher Marlowe - dir. Orson Welles - FTP - Maxine Elliott's Theatre, New York

1937: *The Cradle Will Rock* by Marc Blitzstein - dir. Orson Welles - FTP - Venice Theatre, New York

1938: *The Shoemaker's Holiday* by Thomas Dekker, adapt. Orson Welles - dir. Orson Welles - Mercury Theatre company - Mercury Theatre, New York

1938: "Captain Shotover" in *Heartbreak House* by George Bernard Shaw - dir. Orson Welles - Mercury Theatre company - Mercury Theatre, New York

1938: *Too Much Johnson* by William Gillette - dir. Orson Welles - Mercury Theatre company - Stony Creek Summer Theatre, Stony Creek, CT

1938: "Louis Antoine de Saint-Just" in *Danton's Death* by Georg Büchner, adapt. Orson Welles - dir. Orson Welles - Mercury Theatre company - Mercury Theatre, New York

1939: "Falstaff" in *Five Kings* (Part One) by Orson Welles, adapt. from *Richard II*; *Henry IV, Parts I* and *II*; and *Henry V* by William Shakespeare - dir. Orson Welles - Theatre Guild / Mercury Theatre company - Colonial Theatre, Boston

1941: *Native Son* by Paul Green and Richard Wright, adapt. from the novel by Wright - dir. Orson Welles - Mercury Theatre company - St. James Theatre, New York

1943: "Orson the Magnificent" in *The Mercury Wonder Show for Service Men* - dir. Orson Welles - Mercury Theatre company - Mercury Wonder Show Tent, Los Angeles

1946: "Dick Fix" in *Around the World* by Orson Welles and Cole Porter, adapt. from *Around the World in Eighty Days* by Jules Verne - Mercury Productions - Boston Opera House, Boston

1947: "Macbeth" in *Macbeth* by William Shakespeare, adapt. Orson Welles - dir. Orson Welles - Mercury Productions / Utah Centennial Commission and University Theatre - Kingsbury Hall, Salt Lake City, UT

1950: Multiple roles in *The Blessed and the Damned* (a.k.a. *Time Runs*, or *The Unthinking Lobster*) by Orson Welles - dir. Orson Welles - Les Pleiades company - Théâtre Édouard VII, Paris

1951: "Othello" in *Othello* by William Shakespeare, adapt. Orson Welles - dir. Orson Welles - Theatre Royal, Newcastle upon Tyne, UK

1953: *The Lady in the Ice* (a.k.a. *Une femme dans la glace*) by Orson Welles and Jean-Michel Damase - dir. Orson Welles - chor. Roland Petit - Ballet de Paris - Stoll Theatre, London

1955: Multiple roles in *Moby Dick—Rehearsed* by Orson Welles, adapt. from the novel by Herman Melville - dir. Orson Welles - Duke of York's Theatre, London

1956: "Lear" in *King Lear* by William Shakespeare, adapt. Orson Welles - dir. Orson Welles - New York City Center Theatre Company - New York City Center Theater, New York

1960: "Sir John Falstaff" in *Chimes at Midnight* by Orson Welles, adapt. from *Henry IV, Parts I* and *II*; *Henry V*; *Richard II*; and *The Merry Wives of Windsor* by William Shakespeare - dir. Hilton Edwards - Gate Theatre Company - Grand Opera House, Belfast, Ireland

1960: *Rhinoceros* by Eugène Ionesco, trans. Derek Prouse - dir. Orson Welles - English Stage Company - Royal Court Theatre, London

Radio credits (non-exhaustive)

1934: *The American School of the Air* (voice, CBS)

1935–1938: *The March of Time* (voice, CBS)

1935: *America's Hour* (voice, CBS)

1936: *The Wonder Show* (voice, Mutual Broadcasting System)

1936–1938: *Columbia Workshop* (voice, writer; CBS)

1937: *Les Misérables* (voice, writer, director; Mutual)

1937–1938: *The Shadow* (voice, Mutual)

1938–1940: *The Mercury Theatre on the Air*, a.k.a. *The Campbell Playhouse* (voice, writer, director, producer; CBS)

1938: *The Silver Theatre* (voice, CBS)

1941–1942: *The Orson Welles Show* (voice, writer, director, producer; CBS); *The Cavalcade of America* (voice, NBC Red)

1942–1944: *Suspense* (voice, CBS)

1942–1943: *Ceiling Unlimited* (voice, writer, director, producer; CBS); *Hello Americans* (voice, writer, director, producer; CBS)

1943: *Treasury Star Parade* (voice; US Treasury Department, syndicated)

1943–1947: *Command Performance* (voice, American Forces Network)

1944: *The Orson Welles Almanac* (voice, writer, director; CBS); *The Fifth War Loan Drive* (voice, writer, director, producer; US Treasury Department, syndicated)

1944–1945: *This Is My Best* (voice, writer, director, producer; CBS)

1945: *The Free World Forum* (moderator, Blue Network)

1945–1946: *Orson Welles Commentaries* (voice, writer, director, producer; ABC)

1951–1952: *The Adventures of Harry Lime* (voice, writer; syndicated)

1951–1952: *The Black Museum* (voice, syndicated)

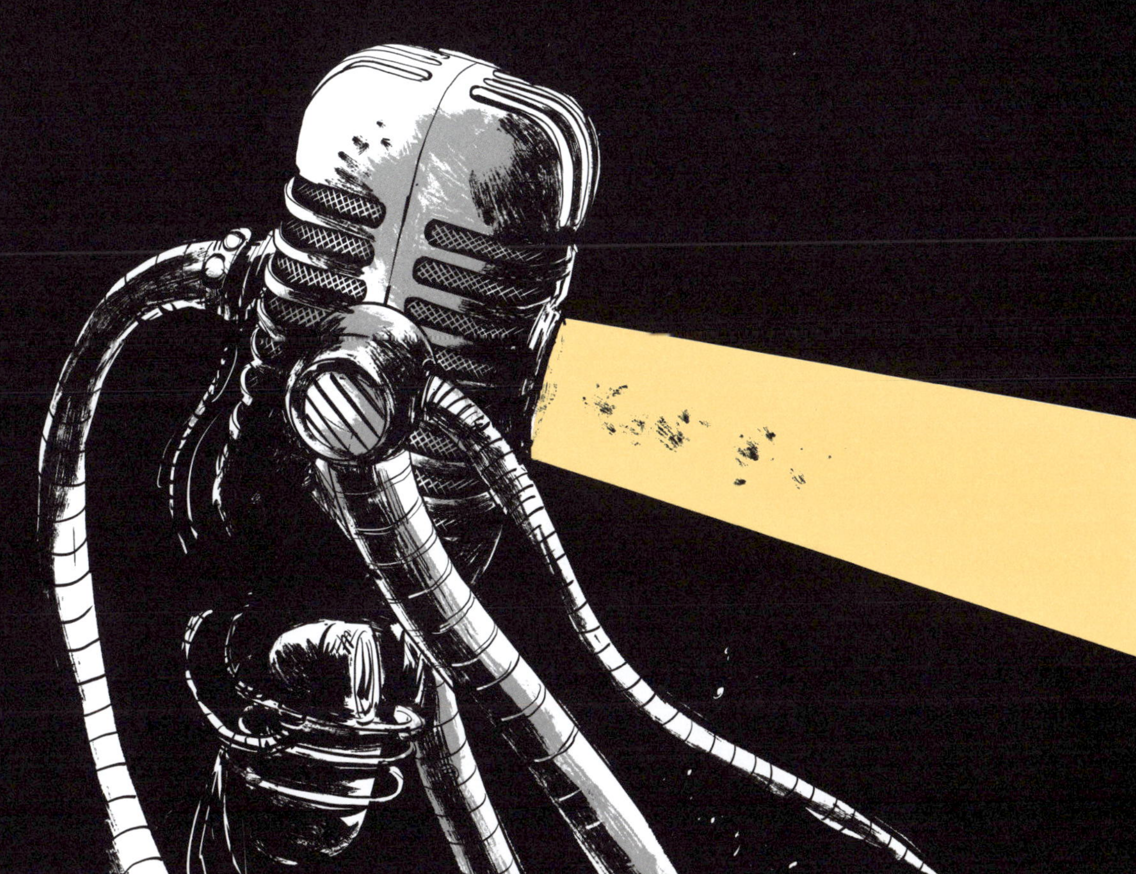

Your fresh start
in great graphic novels.

For young readers of all ages.

Your one stop
in great comics.

For grown-ups.

Published by 23rd St.
23rd Street is an imprint of Roaring Brook Press, a division of Holtzbrinck Publishing Holdings Limited Partnership
120 Broadway, New York, NY 10271
23rdstbooks.com • firstsecondbooks.com

Library of Congress Control Number: 2023948782

First edition, 2025 • Edited by Mark Siegel and Tess Banta • Cover design by Kirk Benshoff and Yan L. Moy
Interior book design by Sunny Lee and Yan L. Moy • Production editing by Sarah Gompper

Drawn with traditional and digital media using carbon ink on Canson paper and a Cintiq 22HD tablet with Clip Studio Paint 2.0 and custom ink pen and dry brushes. Lettered digitally with the Orson Regular font, designed especially for this book by the author.

Printed in China

ISBN 978-1-250-80594-2
1 3 5 7 9 10 8 6 4 2